TEAM BRIEFING

TEAM BRIEFING

A PRACTICAL HANDBOOK

Phil McGeough

The Industrial Society

First published in 1995 by
The Industrial Society
Robert Hyde House
48 Bryanston Square
London W1H 7LN
Telephone: 0171–262 2401

© The Industrial Society 1995

ISBN 1 85835 144 8

British Library Cataloguing-in-Publication Data.
A catalogue record for this book is available from the
British Library

Typeset by: Midlands Book Typesetting Company, Loughborough
Printed by: Lavenham Press
Cover design: Integra Communications

Text cartoons: Martin Shovel

The Industrial Society is a registered charity no. 290003

ACKNOWLEDGEMENTS

I gratefully acknowledge my colleagues at The Industrial Society for their thoughts and expertise, which helped me to produce this book.

In particular I wish to thank Andy Garnett, Jacqui Pattison, Bob Shiers and Paul Davis for sharing with me their experience and good humour.

CONTENTS

INTRODUCTION

There has been a great increase in interest in employee communications in recent years. It seems to spring partly from the age old need to minimise misunderstandings and engage people's enthusiasm for the organisation's goals. It is also related to the need to give good customer care by ensuring that employees feel themselves well-informed, cared for and able effectively to feed back ideas or problems to decision-makers.

The Industrial Society has been campaigning for effective employee communication since the 1920s. We are constantly learning more about how successful organisations evolve their communication. One of the consistent features we find is that they use systematic and regular management communication as a cornerstone. Team briefing is the classic way of conducting management communication. Our recent survey (Feb 1994) of 915 organisations, showed team briefing rated by far the most effective channel to employees. Employee surveys, too, show a consistent preference for face to face communication from line managers.

This book is a guide to Team Briefing, built on the experience of successful organisations evolving their systems into the mid 90s.

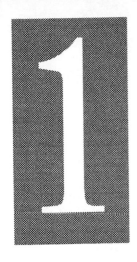

THE COMMUNICATIONS PROBLEM

Communicating with the workforce shouldn't be a complicated, contentious business, but there is evidence that it is.

It is not unreasonable to imagine that as the performance, successes, intentions or aspirations of an organisation need to be explained to everyone, it is a fairly straightforward matter of sending round a circular or putting a note on the notice board. On the other hand, we could print something in the company house journal, or even ask managers to tell their staff.

The purpose of communication is to create understanding in the mind(s) of others, but, for many organisations, just how much understanding is being created is a matter of conjecture. In the case of very major topics, the importance of communication becomes spotlighted. Crises, major change and unusual business developments seem to cause exceptionally good internal communications – in both directions. They also seem to reveal the fact that, under more normal business conditions, communication is haphazard and inconsistently managed.

What is often then highlighted is the reality that, when internal communications are put under the microscope, there are a number of specific things which need to be addressed and put right.

Managers are all too easily blamed for the so-called 'communications problem'. After all, they are the ones who are supposedly all knowing. Unfortunately, if we make this assumption, it may well be far from the truth. Those 'in management' aren't necessarily any wiser than the staff who report to them. Consequently when junior managers do not appear to have answers to the important questions, the call goes up to 'get "the management" down here to tell us'. Even worse, if people perceive that junior or middle managers don't possess certain information, then it can become a cynical case of, 'it's no use asking him/her anything.' Management credibility is then brought into question.

It is inequitable to put it all down to ineptitude on the part of individual managers, unless they have been told to pass on some information and it hasn't happened. The main inadequacy is that there is probably no controlled process of promulgation and dissemination as a matter of routine.

Whilst the workforce can ultimately highlight the need to put internal communications in order, often it is the most senior group of managers who believe that something should be done to bring about improvements. It is **their** collective frustration which causes discontent and brings about the call for intervention.

STAFF ATTITUDES

Over the last decade there has also been an increase in the use of Staff Opinion Surveys. These are designed to elicit from employees their thoughts about all manner of corporate issues. Very often what is elicited is an unequivocal condemnation of the ways in which an organisation manages, or rather fails to manage, internal communications.

A newly appointed managing director once confided to me that the results of an Attitude Survey proved, amongst other things, that in his company, all sorts of management controls were being managed to the nth degree. Procedures and finely detailed processes were in place to make the business run smoothly. But the most important aspect of that business had been left to chance. Communication, he said, was an unmanaged hit and miss shambles and it left him with no guaranteed means of disseminating important information to all the levels below. This is something we hear regularly. Like everything else in business, communication needs to be managed.

More sophisticated means of communicating have added to the problem. As individuals we are almost spoilt for choice in terms of the medium for communication. Quite apart from the obvious ways such as face-to-face or the inevitable piece of paper, we now have the fax machine, teleconferencing, electronic mail, business television, cordless mobile phones and audio voicemail. The information super highway is no longer a fanciful dream. Communicating on a one-to-one basis has never been easier, but have these things really brought about any significant overall improvements in relation to corporate communications with people?

Asking the staff what they think about their organisation's standards of internal communication can be very revealing. Rarely do they say anything complimentary. If for example we ask how often or regularly they go to any team based meeting, the response is all too frequently '. . . well, sometimes', 'We have them as and when', or 'We're supposed to have them every month, but they keep on postponing or cancelling them.'

Naturally, it goes without saying that managers, and that means anyone who is seen to be 'in charge', are constantly communicating to create understanding. It's happening all the time and it is primary and fundamental to the job. In fact, it goes with the job.

So why all the condemnation? Why the perception that we aren't doing enough to keep people informed, that communication is for some and not for others, or that the 'need to know' syndrome still prevails in a number of organisations? The answers are not particularly complex, but we need to go back to basics.

It is all very well determining through whatever means that there is an internal communication problem. There are almost certainly communication problems in every organisation. Determining what specific problems are perceived (that word again) to exist is vital before any remedial action can be taken.

There is a list of specific issues which seems to crop up time and time again. Some are hoary old chestnuts but remain important because they are. Others are less obvious. This is the list compiled, for the most part, from listening to people at the front edge of organisations.

- Blockages

- Filtering

- Clouded issues

- 'Can't find out'

- Irrelevant information

- Different stories

- Different versions of stories at different times

- Lack of why

- Insufficient or incoherent financial statements

- Historical information

- Invisible management

- Rumour, speculation, the grapevine

- Secrecy/confidentiality

- 'We weren't told'

- Lack of understandable news

- Assumed knowledge/understanding

- Inconsistency
- 'As and when' meetings
- Meetings cancelled/postponed
- No upwards feedback
- Selective dissemination
- Misunderstandings

For some a natural reaction to this formidable list is that however hard we try, people like to have a moan and whinge at every given opportunity. This view assumes the worst of mankind. We sometimes hear more senior people say that their staff like a 'good old wallow' and that their working day wouldn't be complete without one. Doubtless some people are more gloomy than others, but of one thing I am certain, I have never yet met anyone in the world of work who sets out intentionally to do a bad job. People want to do a good job and want success, both for themselves and for the organisation. It seems unlikely that the perceived communication problems help either of these things to come about.

In management we can deny, emphatically if necessary, that the list is true or valid. To do so would be to miss the point, which is that if these are the things which are perceived to be true, then that is what has to be managed.

Some analysis of the raw list is important.

Blockages: Important information reaches more senior people but doesn't get passed on. This also gives rise to a perception that, for some, 'knowledge is power'.

Filtering: A belief that to suit the mood or whim of any manager, key messages are left out of dissemination. During times when any bad news is going around and despite the intention of senior management to impart whatever it is, managers lower down remove or modify the messages. They say that to pass them on would do more harm than good.

Editing in this way is arguably well intentioned, but that is not the way it is viewed by the majority of staff.

Interestingly, a very senior person within GEC had a different slant on this subject. He said that one of the major anxieties of being one of the top people is constantly wondering what messages or news items are being filtered on the way up through the layers. Filtering is at least as important a problem in upward communication.

Clouded Issues: 'We know something is going on', people often tell me. 'They don't want us to know,' is what they say. 'Confusing smoke signals' is the way another put it to me. On taking a closer look at this issue, very often there isn't any intention to conceal information or misinform. It's sometimes the usual business of individuals hearing just part of a story, passing on what they've heard, or rather what they believe they have heard, and others second guessing in order to complete a fuzzy picture. When that picture appears to make no sense then the perception is that decision-makers are deliberately trying to confuse.

This is particularly the case where the messages seem to bear little relation to the world employees see everyday.

'Can't find out': People are naturally inquisitive. When they learn that there is substance to a rumour for example, they are inclined to ask questions.

'We've asked and asked but they're all tight-lipped,' is the way a small team in one insurance company described it. 'We just can't find out what's going on.'

Often, no final decision has been taken, and nothing has been communicated because there are fears of worrying people unnecessarily. On other occasions, it simply has not occurred to the decision-makers that other people would be interested in knowing. This scenario also highlights the old problem of a team's immediate line manager not knowing something of importance in connection with a team for whom he or she is responsible.

When a specific issue of this kind was subsequently queried through the line above the team, there were two surprises. The team supervisor responded that it was pointless asking him because he was no wiser than the team! His manager was much more forthcoming. She explained the issue and was stunned that the supervisor and his team seemingly knew nothing. 'They only had to ask,' she said.

This also highlights the whole business of reactive versus proactive communication which is a vitally important matter in the context of creating understanding.

Irrelevant Information: Any information which is viewed as having no direct bearing on any given group or team of people can come under this heading. Even telling people the good news, that output has increased, that market share has dramatically improved or profits are at record levels, will not necessarily bring about any positive reaction unless we also tell them what it means to them. This also applies to broad praise for everyone for their efforts in bringing about any given state of corporate euphoria. It will miss the target unless we tell people specifically what their particular contribution was. A wide ranging vote of thanks to the staff is rarely enough. It is also unimaginative.

Those in office based jobs will empathise with the views of a manager who informed me that he needs to allocate about five hours every week simply to reading through seemingly endless papers. Many of them are sent 'for information'. Everything from memoranda through to copies of minutes of meetings, computer print-outs, newspaper or magazine clippings, staff notices, competitor information, reports, updates on a whole host of issues and performance data. 'To bin or not to bin, that is the question,' he said. He added that he was slightly puzzled to be told that arrangements had been made for him to attend a Time Management training course.

Most of the paper had been sent on a 'need to know' basis. However, some of it was 'should know' and some of it sent on a 'might possibly, conceivably/be vaguely of value/interest' basis. As the manager also said, it's often sent by people trying to cover themselves or trying to look busy and justify their existence.

Unless we point out the relevance of any paper to individuals, specifically and unequivocally, then both paper and time is wasted. These are serious resource issues.

Junk Mail

Junk mail is bad enough at home without extending it to the workplace. If we take the trouble to send a piece of paper to someone, we should also take the trouble to tell them why it's being sent. All too frequently it's done because someone thinks that someone else just might be interested.

This can lead to more senior people believing, perhaps wrongly, that they have created understanding by bombarding their managers with paper. Even worse perhaps, they also assume that managers are passing the information onward to their teams. This is not always the case and can give rise to the blockages or filtering perceptions.

In relation to oral statements, the method people most prefer according to all the informed research, we can also waste valuable time telling people things which they find irrelevant. That is also a wasted opportunity.

Surely we need to think in terms of three things: what people need to know, (of course), what people would like to know, and also what we would like people to know, understand, and why.

Different Stories: This is the age old matter of people having different versions of the same story. It is frustrating for these people when they compare what they have heard or misheard, or convey to others what they think they have heard.

Different Versions of Stories at Different Times: In the absence of a synchronised formula for promulgation this is inevitabable. If, for example, some people are having meetings while others aren't, then the outfall from the meetings will, at the very least, reach the ears of some of those who did not go to one.

If in addition disparate teams are meeting sometimes in different geographical locations in an unco-ordinated way, then the problem is compounded. Casual encounters at photocopiers and vending machines provide the perfect opportunity for people to reveal to others what they believe is happening, or not, as the case may be. The telephone lines buzz in an attempt by the informed to put the uninformed in the picture. And the staff restaurant or rest rooms provide the same opportunity.

There is kudos to be had for those who can claim to have been first to break any important news to their peers. In their eagerness to earn the kudos total accuracy can be a secondary consideration.

Lack of Why: Telling people what, who, when, where and how is fine and commendable. But telling them *why* something is going on or needs to be done is imperative. 'My labour is for sale, but my heart and mind aren't' is true for many people. I'm not sure to whom we can attribute this ageless truism, but it must surely be the ultimate reason why people need to understand rationale.

We cannot win people's commitment unless we explain the why.

Insufficient or Incoherent Financial Statements: I once sat in on the briefing of a middle manager in a large financial institution. The company were having problems with their Team Briefing and were seeking improvements.

When it came to the all important update on the departmental financial position, the manager said:

'The adversarial downturn in the third quarter is directly equated to the revised expectation in our modified budget (£1.4 million), which is remarkably similar to the upturn at this time last year. I'm sure you will agree this is good news.'

Looking around at the faces of the staff, their blank expressions were unsurprising. There were no questions.

Please do not waste your time trying to make sense of his statement because it isn't possible to do so.

In most organisations there exists a policy and willingness to disclose at least some financial information to staff at all levels. The opportunity is there to keep people informed regularly, and not only once a year in the Annual Report. How this is done and the language we choose are both of primary importance.

Called in to another company by the H.R. director to begin planning the implementation of Team Briefing, I asked why he wanted to use Briefing. I expected the usual response about communication problems. Instead he replied that the directors wanted everyone in the company '. . . to feel closer to the money.' They wanted to heighten awareness about pricing, competitiveness and of course costs and profits and their relevance to the entire workforce. They intended to rid the organisation of past secrecies and become wholly open about the financial affairs.

The Balance Sheet Barrier: Realistically, not everyone can comprehend a financial balance sheet produced by accountants, so if we want to create more understanding about the financial position, then the language has to be modified. Even words like, for example, 'budget', 'contribution' or 'surplus' need clarification and it is a mistake to assume understanding outside financial circles.

Another point worth bearing in mind is that people want to know how the organisation is doing.

Historical Information: People are far less likely to be interested in what happened last week or three months ago, than in the future. What is likely to happen or what is planned to happen are part of an organisation's vital signs and are indications that management is looking ahead and anticipating.

Invisible Management: On a list of communication problems, perhaps the accusation that management is 'faceless' or 'invisible' seems out of place. It's often puzzled me too, but clearly people do make a connection between the apparent lack of management visibility and the communication problem.

This is almost certainly one of those oblique accusations that senior people don't really know what's going on in the everyday workplace because they simply don't visit enough.

Good managers walk-the-job and they do so regularly. They put time aside in their diaries and plan to do it. It is well-intentioned and not aimed at catching people out or keeping people on their toes. They enquire and show interest through chatting briefly with various people at different levels.

In one particular institution where I was working, a few members of staff were complaining to me that they had never once seen their Chief Executive. They had apparently been told that he was a shy man and would feel uncomfortable talking to people.

I revisited the company many months later and learned that the CE had finally undertaken a walkabout. The staff could recall four things about the event. They informed me that he had been flanked by no fewer than four of his directors, that he spoke to no one below manager level, that for two weeks before the event a great deal of tidying up and repainting had been undertaken, and that he was '. . . a good looking chap.'

How very objective. Remote people are often said to be shy. They are also sometimes regarded as being uncaring or indifferent. That's perception for you.

Rumour, Speculation/the Grapevine: Its fun, sociable and above all a natural human trait to speculate and to pass on to others what is circulating on the grapevine. In every organisation there are rumours.

Corporate rumours are inevitable. But why do they invariably focus upon bad things and are the bastion of woeful tidings? When was the last time you heard anything good about the organisation or the people within it by listening to the grapevine? Rumours tend to accentuate the negative and that is why they can be so damaging, demoralising and demotivating.

An immeasurable quantity of time is wasted because of the grapevine. It is undoubtedly time which we can ill afford to lose and we could put to better use.

The grapevine can be pre-empted. We can disarm and discourage it. We can even ridicule it simply by getting in first, anticipating and confronting it.

Importantly, in some organisations, we have to accept that whatever is being discussed at the higher level can leak out sooner or later. It seems not to matter whether these discussions are deeply pertinent to long term well being or not. There is the possibility of leakage and when that happens bits of a story emerge. It is these bits which get passed on, added to in a biased or prejudicial way, exaggerated and manipulated until the damage is done. Sometimes people are merely guessing on the basis of some unexplained events.

A healthy prolific grapevine can be the symptom of a sick organisation. It also causes peremptory articulation and misrepresentation. We should disagree with those who claim that they can use the grapevine to their advantage. Other means of communicating and influencing exist and are less costly in every sense of the words.

Secrecy/Confidentiality: I used to work for a boss who inspired me. He was a true leader who possessed that wonderful sixth sense, which is the way to manage people successfully. He was most excellent in every way except that he was sometimes one for keeping things to himself. If I queried the nature of the piece of paper he was clutching closely to his chest, he seemed to take joy in saying things like '. . . all will be revealed in the fullness of time.' He was also fond of saying '. . . sorry, old boy, can't tell you; you know how it is.'

Well, I probably never got to know how it was. I imagined this was the stuff of the higher minds and people at my level were not always 'on the list', as my boss liked to call it. I stopped worrying about it all when I once discovered that one of the 'secret' documents was to do with VAT recovery on his monthly dining room expenses!

It seems probable that in all organisations there are secret or confidential discussions and papers. There is perhaps natural anxiety that the issues involved could be of value to competitors or in some way cause damage. Sensitive information has to be safeguarded but an undue obsession with it can be equally damaging.

Quite often, sensitive information which those in middle management believe cannot be disseminated can be revealed. It is a matter of telling people clearly whether or not they may and should do so.

'We Weren't Told': Little elaboration is needed for this very old statement.

If people aren't told about things they should know then the consequences are obvious. Things may not get done, deadlines may get missed, and quality may suffer. Who was accountable for communicating with the people who claim they weren't told something? Almost certainly it was someone in a management position.

Lack of Understandable News: Quite apart from adversarial downturns in the third quarter, the natty jargon of organisations is intriguing. There is absolutely nothing wrong with jargon as long as, when it is used on others, it helps to create understanding.

Some new words which have come my way in recent times include:

- Unitology and unitisation

- Clean page solutions

- Aftermarket

- Empowerment

- Corporate energy

- Corporate leverage

- Downsizing

- Rightsizing

- Upsizing

- Plateauing

- Blue sky scenarios

- 'The package' (redundancy)

- Whitehatting (E. De Bono, factgiving)

- Mapmaking (planning)

- Planned exiting (more redundancy)

- Trolls (the competition)

- De-employ (yet more redundancy)

". . . . . Rightsizing our economic resourcing to match regenerative aspirations is swaying our new cultural embodiment towards aftermarket embellishments."

- Sanitising (cleaning up the act)

- Upskilling (training)

- Downskilling

Organisations have their own unique jargon. People who use it and those who understand it have a sense of belonging. Conversely, those who hear it but don't understand can feel left out. This is a simple communication problem to overcome.

Assumed Knowledge/Understanding: This is one of the top five complaints. It has a relationship with jargon but it goes beyond the language problem. 'The latest position regarding (product) is that lab tests are continuing. Indications are that we are unlikely to have to withdraw it from sale.' These are the words of a young Team Leader briefing her team from a prepared script. 'What was the first position?' came the alarmed reaction of her team members. 'Have we missed something?' There followed a familiar backtracking which finally restored credibility and order.

'It was on all the notice boards,' she said, which goes to prove what an unreliable means of communicating with people the company notice board can be. They are often unmanaged objets d'art. They can include miscellaneous calls for everything from sponsors for staff undertaking heroic marathonic sporting challenges, through to good homes being wanted for newly weaned kittens.

Even when notice boards are used properly as a means of keeping people in the picture, you are rarely to see people queuing up to read what's on them. Nor have we yet seen a notice board answering questions. One day maybe, but not yet.

It is extremely frustrating and time wasting when an update is provided regarding a subject which was not common knowledge in the first place.

Inconsistency: Left to chance or individual preference, managers are likely to choose a method of communication which suits them. That isn't necessarily a bad thing. Some will choose to brief their people face-to-face in connection with something newsworthy or topical. Others will circulate a piece of paper or use the screen.

For managers who are responsible for others in scattered locations, always briefing face-to-face isn't an easy option. However, for those who sit in the same area as their team, sending them a piece of paper which members of the team must initial when seen seems pointless, perhaps even a cop out.

Even for staff all based at the same location, newsgiving is likely to be undertaken in an inconsistent fashion. Some will hear face-to-face, some will read it in circular form and some will read it on the notice board. The probable outcome is that people's understanding will also be on three different levels. Time is then wasted while they then jointly try to reach consensus over what the true meaning might be. This is something which staff are quick to point out.

'As and When' Meetings: I have never entirely understood what 'as and when' means. On balance I think it means that people have meetings as and when there is a need for one, but who determines that need?

If it is the team members who are asking for a meeting it's a clue that they've got something on their collective mind which they feel needs sorting out. Once the sorting out has been achieved at 'as and when' meetings, those meetings often become extended to include the Any Other Business issues. These can cover anything from funny smells to strange draughts and people parking their cars selfishly in the car park.

I totally support any planned forum where staff may express their thoughts and opinions. The so-called hygiene factors are important to people and they need to be dealt with. What I take issue with is when staff meetings are scheduled as a reaction rather than in a planned, regular, proactive way. More to the point, staff also take issue over this basic principle.

If, on the other hand, managers are holding irregular meetings 'as and when' at their own instigation then there is a hint that they are knee jerking or being put under pressure to hold meetings with their staff. By then there can be a backlog of matters to discuss, explain, clarify or consult over along with the possible impression that we are usually in reactive mode and putting down rebellion. It's worth pointing out that finding time to have meetings can *save* time and prevent things from building up.

Meetings Cancelled/Postponed: In management, something crops up and we put off the meeting. Seen through the eyes of the staff, almost any other business matter can take priority over 'routine meetings'. At least that is what we constantly hear.

The point is obvious. Staff meetings are not always seen as an integral part of business and getting the job done better.

No Upwards Feedback: In the main, there are more 'mechanisms' for providing information than there are for people to communicate upwards. Only in rare cases do we find that the organisation possesses means and procedures designed for hearing and listening to the staff at all levels.

Senior managers often say they would like to have more feedback. This is perfectly in line with the people at lower levels who want the opportunity to express themselves. Somewhere between these two points it fails to come about.

Upwards filtering is an obvious problem, perhaps too obvious because that assumes feedback is elicited in the first place, which is not always the case.

Formal consultative arrangements can ensure that there exists some process for constructive dialogue directly between members of staff and senior managers. Suggestion Schemes, Talkback documentation and Quality Improvement Teams can also achieve much in relation to creating understanding upwards. Perhaps it is the absence of these commendable arrangements which tends to throw up the call for improvements in the listening arrangements.

Selective Dissemination: It would be naive to suggest that organisations can always manage their affairs in a totally open manner. Confidentiality and the consequent 'need to know' syndrome will prevail from time to time. Only those in more senior positions can judge whether or not any given degree of selective dissemination is excessive or appropriate.

However, we are back to the issues which recur over and over. If people get wind of issues which have been selectively disseminated, in some organisations speculation in varying degrees occurs, and a firm announcement is needed even if it is not the final story.

This is more likely to be a problem in larger organisations. Distribution lists are compiled and seem to automatically govern who, and at what level, receives what information through the internal mail system. This procedure becomes routine and can result in complaints about irrelevant information reaching people or, more importantly, relevant information *not* reaching people.

Misunderstandings: Misunderstandings can be minor but equally they can be a serious matter. They can cause uncertainty and frustration. They seem all too easily trivialised and dismissed as '. . . just a misunderstanding'. Unfortunately they can actually prevent things from happening as planned and of course cause things to happen which shouldn't. The result is always wasted time; and time is money.

It seems highly unlikely that in an organisation every one of these specific communication problems can exist. However, it is important to bear in mind that whatever problems there are in any organisation, there are natural and obvious consequences.

They undermine the credibility of managers.
They undermine the credibility of the organisation.
They impede progress and the ability to get the job done.
Precious time is wasted.
Negativity and indifference prevail.

It is also vitally important to understand that there is no quick fix and no individual formula which will eradicate all communication problems. Things will improve only if there is a fundamental determination to overcome them along with a willingness to disclose information and then to target it so that people are getting relevant information. In other words, through managing communications and applying certain codes of practice in a disciplined way. These are essential matters if we are to begin to overcome the perceived problems.

- If within an organisation there is a belief that internal communications are messy, unco-ordinated and, in extreme cases, left to chance, then an important first step is to undertake some kind of **audit/survey** to establish what the particular problems are.

- The call for **continuous improvement** and quality management has also spotlighted internal communications as something which needs to be standardised and proceduralised so that conformance can be determined.

- Yet another motive for bringing about improvements is the belief that through better communication we can actually **involve people** more. People cannot begin to feel involved unless they understand what is going on and the effects upon them as individuals and teams.

- The **Investors in People** initiative has further highlighted the need to ensure that people understand core values and missions. It also causes focus upon the maximisation of the human resource contributions *and* their involvement, to an organisation's well-being.

Whatever the motive for wanting to create more understanding, in wanting improvement, one thing is certain. Time and effort will need to be expended. Some corporate energy will have to be rechannelled to make it happen.

CULTURE & OBJECTIVITY

Creating the understanding is a major challenge in management today and it is far from being a simple matter. First and foremost it is important to regard communication as something which needs to be managed because the penalties for not doing so can cause some of the extreme difficulties already summarised in this chapter.

Managing communications is also a cultural issue. It is no use pretending that an autocratic, 'need to know' type of organisation will ever find a process of communication easy to manage or maintain. Their inherent and entrenched cultural instincts will always get in the way. However, if these *Theory 'X'* organisations are determined to move towards the principles of staff involvement, then more openness, dialogue and disclosure are essentials in that shift.

In those organisations in which there is already greater democracy and belief that *through* people, so much more can be achieved, effective communications are usually at the heart of everything. Getting communications right to actually help the organisation get to where it wants to be is regarded as fundamental.

If we want to harness the abilities of our people then they need to understand both the imperatives and the aspirations. It's as simple as that. And it's a mistake to believe that we can motivate people solely with pieces of paper. Nor can we reasonably expect to do so while our people have grievances, ideas, or problems which they are never able to air or get resolved. They will be out of focus with the core values and missions however highly prized and publiced these might be.

METHODS & CHANNELS

The methods and channels for communication in organisations need to be defined and used selectively to achieve different things. If we understand the nature of each method then clearly we have a greater chance of choosing the correct one objectively.

It is important to differentiate between the three distinct internal channels.

They are, DOWNWARD, UPWARD and LATERAL.

The **Downward** channel can involve the following methods:

Face to Face
- Team Meetings
- Team Briefings
- One-to-One's
- Appraisals
- Conferences
- Presentations/Roadshows
- Induction
- Product Launch Previews

Non Face-to-Face
- Teleconferencing
- House Journals/News Letters
- Videofilms
- Memoranda
- Electronic Mail
- Audiotaping
- Business Television
- Employee Annual Reports
- Publicity & Promotional material
- Employee Handbooks
- Procedural Notes

The **Upward** methods are:
- Consultative Committee Meetings
- Unions and other representative body meetings
- Quality Improvement Teams
- Suggestion Schemes
- Speak Up Programmes
- Team Briefing Feedback
- Appraisals

- Attitude Surveys

- Managers 'walking the job'

- Customer Liaison Meetings

The **lateral** communication channels could include:

- Peer Meetings/Conferences (including teleconferencing)

- Project Meetings

- Team Briefing Drill

- Joint Training

- Task Forces

- Director Lunches

- Cross Functional Quality Teams

- Electronic Mail

- Guest Speakers at Team Meetings

TEAM BRIEFING features in all three internal channels, which is probably one of the reasons for its remarkable popularity in today's world of work. If it is used as part of an overall strategy to work to manage communications in conjunction with other mediums then Team Briefing offers very significant potential.

Team Briefing can be the cornerstone of an organisation's internal communications programme. It is often seen as vital because it is unlikely that upward or lateral communications can work as effectively as they might unless the downward channel is first working well to create understanding. Consultative Committees, for example, cannot be truly effective unless those involved have a clear understanding of the issues about which there are to be consultations.

Whether in the public or private sectors, large or small, whether it is involved in manufacturing, retail, service, production, process, education or charitable work, in most organisations Team Briefing can work to help create the dialogue. This can be crucial in bringing about success.

WHAT IS TEAM BRIEFING?

TEAM COMMUNICATION

In management we achieve the task through those who work for us. An integral part of managing a group of people is to encourage and develop team identity and teamwork. People need to understand common goals and the work realities if they are to be an effective team. Communication is a vital part of achieving team success. It is inconceivable that there can be any continuous team success unless someone is regularly talking to the team, face-to-face, and that is the responsibility of line management.

All modern research proves conclusively that people prefer, whenever possible, to hear about issues that affect them face–to–face. This should come as no surprise. We cannot ask questions of a piece of paper. We cannot see people's reactions nor accurately judge their responses unless we are there with them. No written words of encouragement can ever have the same impact as someone saying them face–to–face. Voice recordings and videos will do much good but still, by their very nature, disallow questions and the simple opportunity for clarification.

Communicating with the team is part of any manager's job. You do not have to be particularly gifted or talented to be able to communicate with the team and using your own every day language is far better than using someone else's.

OBJECTIVES

Team Briefing is a process of face-to-face communication using a simple synchronised formula. Leaders at all levels gather their people together in their respective teams on a regular timetabled basis and brief them for about half an hour. Part of the arrangement involves doing so throughout any organisation within a short specified time frame – perhaps within two or three days. Another important part of the process is that it includes and involves everyone through their teams.

BACKGROUND

There is absolutely nothing new in members of management meeting their teams and talking to them. It is said that the invading Roman armies used a form of briefing in their battle units. Sports teams invariably receive the customary pre-match and half-time team talk aimed at tactical success. The Bible has it that Moses briefed his people, having first been briefed by God and given 'the brief' in hard form!

BRIEFING GROUPS

Thirty or so years ago 'Briefing Groups' were inaugurated in industry. These were top down arrangements used to cascade information through the layers to everyone. This early form of briefing became modified, improved, developed and has therefore evolved and indeed continue to evolve.

The problem with Briefing Groups was that they were firmly based on the notion that people at every level are always riveted and motivated by messages reaching them from the very top of the organisation. The evidence suggests they are not.

Statements of excellent profits, improved market share and all kinds of corporate well being are, of course, important. Telling people how well the current reorganisation is going can be an important statement too. The same applies to our business plans, marketing direction, capital investment, news of new products or company policy. They are the life blood of the organisation and we are driven by them. But unless everyone understands such things from the perspective of their own work, these messages can be perceived as sterile. People want to understand the relevance of such matters in relation to individuals and the team.

Briefing Groups ultimately depended for their success upon members of senior management imaginatively creating messages of interest and encouragement to be cascaded. When that novelty wore off and when they simply ran out of things to say, Briefing Groups were widely sidelined or under utilised. Only those who by then had identified the essential missing ingredient, namely LOCALISED INFORMATION, continued to feel benefit in their briefing arrangements.

Team Briefing evolved directly from Briefing Groups. A director from a major chemical company put it to me very succinctly. He said that Briefing Groups had reached the point where it would have been more sensible to invest in a hundred or so audio tape players and for taped messages from the directorate to be played to the assembled groups. Just as much would have been achieved, he said, and something had to change.

Perhaps it was in those organisations which were by then listening to their people, that there was the timely realisation that by *localising* information there was a sense of involvement and that communication problems were being overcome. Certainly by managers and team leaders adding to the all important directorate 'core' statements, and implanting news and updates which had a direct bearing upon the teams, there was the creation of understanding and enlightenment, along with less rumour and speculation.

CONTEMPORARY TEAM BRIEFING

Team Briefing today still includes the cascade of important statements from the Chief Executive. These are the 'core management' messages which continue to go to everyone. However, vitally, they are no longer the only focus of attention in briefing.

Briefing the team is something which good managers have been doing for a very long time. Team Briefing is not going to solve all the communication problems overnight. Many other forms of communication exist and should be used (please, not the grapevine), selectively, to achieve other things.

Team Briefing has a unique flavour and distinctive characteristics. For example a TEAM MEETING is more discussion orientated and can often be covered in the same forum as team briefing. Team Briefing has evolved out of what can actually work in practice rather than any theoretical, notional, judgement. It is a simple process based upon six basic principles. These are that it is:

- **Face-to-face**

- **In Teams**

- **By the Team Leader**

- **On a Regular Basis**

- **About Relevant Issues**

- **Monitored**

- **An Opportunity for Feedback**

If any one of these six components is missing, then Team Briefing is weakened or it can no longer realistically be regarded as Team Briefing.

Because Team Briefing is such a simple concept, there is the temptation to try to sophisticate it in some way.

This is unwarranted. There are no rules cast in tablets of stone which have to be slavishly adhered to, but there are uncomplicated guidelines based on what makes sense and what others have already experienced and found to work. Another important point to remember is that the success of Team Briefing also depends upon the enthusiasm of Briefers themselves, as opposed to the design of the process.

The word 'briefing' is perhaps self explanatory. Images of people briefing the Press are conjured up. It is to do with explaining, stating the position, clarifying and putting one's points across to a group of people. In order to achieve full understanding, questions are answered and speculation avoided.

In connection with Team Briefing that is precisely it.

The word 'briefing' also contains the adjective 'brief'. To be brief implies brevity – of short duration. This too applies to Team Briefing. Briefing one's team should not take hours. In most cases, twenty to forty minutes is quite sufficient.

THE TITLE

Team Briefing is not a purist title for the process. Some senior people simply prefer to use a different term to describe it. Just as long as it incorporates the six principles, they should call it whatever seems suitable.

In some organisations Team Briefing has faltered or failed completely and attempts have then been made to renew it. When this happens it is tempting to give it a new name, in the belief that it can be thought of as different from something which has a tarnished image.

Sometimes, organisations merely prefer their own home grown title.

In some notable cases, Team Briefing is known as, for example:

- Team Talk
- Newstalk
- Communication Groups
- News Brief
- Update Groups
- Team Forum

Using the simple formula, every manager or team leader is required – regularly – to get the team together and to provide factual information to them. In order for them to do so effectively and not feel vulnerable, Briefers must first be briefed by their respective line managers.

Vulnerability is an important word in the context of Team Briefing. One of the key reasons why some managers do not hold meetings – or do so only 'as and when' – is because they can feel vulnerable. They feel uncomfortable because they do not necessarily have answers to give to questions from the team. They might also worry that they do not have 'approval' to impart certain information. This vulnerability can be overcome by briefing managers before they go off to brief their teams.

By doing this simple thing, managers at all levels have the chance to receive oral statements from decision-makers and to fully understand them before passing them onwards. By also having the statements in written form, and through questioning, the inside story concerning any particular matter can be obtained. Managers may then feel confident and even enthusiastic about their roles as key communicators.

Briefing is sometimes equated to a relay race. The starting gun is fired and four runners have each to run their leg of the race and pass on the baton to one another. As the baton is passed on at the end/beginning of each leg there is a brief coming together of two of the runners. In Team Briefing, the number of batons (briefing documents) accumulates, so that the person who 'runs' the final leg may be carrying three or four.

The runners' commitment to the task is another important analogy and dropping the baton at any point along the way means that the task is incomplete. The duration of the race could be regarded as the timescale or 'cycle' of briefing – not that it should be measured in minutes.

The analogy also highlights the discipline and drill of Team Briefing. Later passages of this book describe these in greater detail and define the necessary steps to gain proficiency.

FEARS

It is a mistake to assume that all managers will willingly and enthusiastically brief their teams. The briefing formula has to insist that no 'leg' of the process is missed out and so managers are **caused** to undertake briefing. Some may do so reluctantly.

The point here is that on a list of *Homo sapiens'* fears we have lifts, flying, insects and spiders, deep water, sickness and death, snakes, heights and so on. Public speaking is invariably the number one declared fear. It comes a long way ahead of sickness and death, which seems to suggest that some people would rather die than speak to a gathering or assembly.

If managers perceive that what Team Briefing requires of them is to give a public speech, then some will run a mile in the wrong direction. It has to be put into sensible perspective. Team Briefing requires managers and team leaders to sit down with the team and talk. No one has to give a speech. And no one wants to feel that he or she is talking to the team in isolation. If everyone in management is doing it at around the same time then it doesn't feel so bad.

THE BENEFITS

In organisations where Team Briefing works we may expect significant benefits, including some which organisations seem constantly to be striving for but which always seem just out of reach.

We should be suspicious of extravagant claims for Team Briefing, but listen carefully to those who go to the trouble to take before and after pictures of their organisations. If a communication survey undertaken prior to the introduction of Team Briefing cites specific problems, then six months later when Team Briefing has bedded down, another survey will be revealing.

The benefits include:

SPECIFIC COMMUNICATION PROBLEMS SOLVED

Team Briefing will not solve them all. But if we know in advance what needs to be improved, then we have a good chance of addressing it through Team Briefing.

This can mean an end to blockages, filtering or different versions of different stories for different people. It can cause the decline of out-of-control rumouring, and managers will be seen to be leading.

Team Briefing can do what we want it to do.

REDUCES THE FEAR OF CHANGE

For many people change is not seen as something to be embraced. For example, new technology has taken away thousands of jobs over the years. Shrinking markets, increased competition, restructuring, diversification, new products and the abandonment of old ways of doing things can seem threatening.

Team Briefing can be used to explain the significance and proportion of change. After all, we live in a changing world where nothing remains the same for long. Organisations are having to change and change is here to stay.

Ensuring that people understand change and how it is being managed will help them to co-operate and accept their parts in making it happen.

IT HELPS TO BUILD TEAMS

Team Briefing alone cannot achieve this, but it will help immeasurably. A great deal is spoken and written about team spirit and team synergy. There is a justified belief that people like to feel part of a team. Briefing the team members together as a team can do much to establish and sustain team identity.

IMPROVED COMMITMENT

We cannot measure people's commitment. The best we can do is to look at their performance, determination, flexibility, enthusiasm and willingness. These can signal levels of commitment. Winning people's commitment and the added value this can bring to an organisation is another major challenge in management, and we cannot begin to do so without effective communication. Team Briefing provides one of the primary means.

Acknowledge team success.

GREATER FINANCIAL AWARENESS

Raw statistics can be extremely dull. People want to know the overall financial performance of the organisation but not uninspiring lectures.

I have seen some excellent portrayals of financial and statistical information using simple graphics, bar charts, pie charts or line graphs, for example. Compiling these has never been simpler. Desk top computers can provide all the options.

Two obvious warnings are:

- avoid spending excessive time at Team Briefings explaining the intricacies of accounting;

- avoid unnecessary jargon.

CLEARER OBJECTIVES

Regularly reminding people of the major objectives which drive any business along is essential. It is a mistake to assume that they know. Further down, divisional, departmental and team objectives are different and not necessarily obvious. People like to know what is being aimed at.

The same applies to the COMMON PURPOSE whatever it may be. Creating the understanding can do nothing but help in achieving our goals.

IMPROVED MORALE

There may be any number of reasons why staff morale is low at any given point in time. Poor morale can lead to other things such as scepticism, cynicism, indifference, apathy and irrational pessimism. It can also induce lower standards of performance.

It would be quite wrong to claim that Team Briefing alone will solve deeply entrenched morale problems. But what it can do is to create dialogue and be used to explain the issues which are causing malaise. Without dialogue nothing much can be done in the short term. Effective communication is the key.

Team Briefing can restore co-operation and bring about more understanding and less misunderstanding. Used sensibly it can disarm and undermine rumour. It can discourage idle gossip and through heightened awareness of whatever is going on, promote unity and therefore improve the overall performance of the enterprise.

IMPROVED CONSULTATION

In many organisations there are separate arrangements for consulting employee representatives. Team briefing can contribute to the quality of consultation, by keeping all employees informed of the issue being consulted and encouraging them to put their views to their representatives. In this way all employees, not just representatives, have a way of influencing decisions and representatives benefit from having the chance to canvass views before attending the meeting.

Team briefing can also be used for local consultation, especially when it has a team meeting attached to it. Where the person taking the meeting can also take the decision, he or she can usefully use the opportunity provided by team briefing to seek the team's view before taking the decision.

CONCLUSION

Above all, effective communication is a business imperative and it is incumbent on leaders to be a principal source of information for their teams. It is also an accountability all too easily relegated from a priority list.

One of the greatest manifestations of management activity is to SEE the leader talking to his or her team. Managers may look busy in their offices or spaces away from the team but that very separation can cause some to wonder what managers do all day. That can be a barrier and cause communication problems.

A significant benefit results from the very act of the leader getting the team together. He or she who communicates – leads. Taking charge of communications means that someone else doesn't. What a benefit that can be.

THE PRINCIPLES

FACE-TO-FACE

Talking to people face-to-face is the only way of ensuring that they have received information and understood. Through mutual questioning misunderstandings are avoided. You can see reactions, the so called non-oral messages, which can often tell us more than the spoken word.

Flattened structures and complex reporting line matrices mean that for some managers their teams are not all in one place. Sales forces and other itinerant staff can also present a problem when it comes to regular briefing. In these cases other measures may sometimes have to be used.

However, there usually exists a plan for disparate or scattered individuals to come together from time to time and that is when they can be briefed as a team. It may not always be possible to brief them face-to-face say twelve times a year, but they should never be excluded from Team Briefing purely on the grounds that, for them, the process cannot always be face-to-face.

I have encountered managers who, during the course of each briefing cycle, travel many miles so that they may brief scattered teams. This is commendable and shows determination. It is all too easy to imagine that it is an impossible task. Usually it isn't. Teams away from what they could regard as 'the centre' are invariably those who are inclined to believe that their communication problems are worse than anyone else's. We should never justify that perception.

THE GEOGRAPHY PROBLEM

In an extreme case, in a particular Insurance company which was establishing Team Briefing, we had to overcome the problem of getting core-messages to eleven regional locations all over the UK. One single senior manager had accountability for all eleven outlets and each of the respective eleven area managers reported directly to the senior manager who was based centrally. A monthly face-to-face briefing was considered too expensive.

We simply used the fax machine at the appropriate moment each month. The faxed messages were sent directly and only to each area manager. A subsequent pre-arranged telephone call to each one ensured the necessary understanding and also allowed a summary of localised information which each area manager would be adding regionally. They now use electronic screen mail to convey the core messages, instead of the faxing arrangement. Other organisations use teleconferencing for the same purpose.

These eleven managers also meet as a team quarterly in a central location for a day long meeting. At each quarterly meeting there is a consolidated Team Briefing on the agenda.

Sometimes we have to settle for what is sensible, least worst, practical and manageable. Better that than nothing at all, or an unmanaged, unco-ordinated arrangement.

In most cases of course, teams actually work together in one place and they are easily identifiable as a unit because of their affinity. And so Team Briefing can almost always be face-to-face.

IN TEAMS

Day-to-day one-to-one communications are a natural part of working in a team. If we add to these the contacts which are constantly being made beyond the sphere of the team, and meetings which the teams manager attends in other parts of the organisation, we can easily see how individual team members have different levels of knowledge and understanding.

Good managers regularly talk to individual team members about the things which are pertinent to the individual. In so doing it is also possible that matters arise which have relevance to the whole team. Telling each team member something separately will almost guarantee different versions of it by virtue of the unique questioning from the individuals.

Team Briefing provides the opportunity to talk to the team as a unit about things which affect them all. The level of understanding is potentially greater. At Team Briefing individuals will ask questions which perhaps the others had not considered. The answers can enlighten everyone in the team, even those shrinking violets who prefer not to question things.

There is also the matter of team synergy and motivation to consider. Team Briefing underlines the value and potential of team working.

The size of the team being briefed must also be addressed. Flattened management structures have brought about increases in some team sizes. Between 3 and 15 in number is ideal. More than 15, and inhibition factors can come into play.

BY THE TEAM LEADER

A Team Leader can be the managing director, a sales manager or someone on the first rung of management. By definition, it is anyone who has, as their direct reports, a team of people.

Usually in the case of a Chief Executive, his or her team comprises a number of directors. At the front end, the team will be hands-on staff directly involved in some kind of task orientated output and managed by a team leader or supervisor.

In the context of Team Briefing, if for example the Marketing Manager were to brief a team of production people, doubtless there would be some understanding and enlightenment. Unfortunately however the manager is unlikely to be an expert on production. He or she may only be broadly familiar with what goes on in the production department and is unlikely therefore to speak their language. Nor can the team talk in professional marketing terms.

Only when the immediate leader of the team talks to them will there be the potential for realistic dialogue. Only the appropriate Team Leader possesses the detailed understanding to articulate directly relevant information and deal with questions, comments and other sorts of feedback.

If very senior people wish to talk directly to front line staff from time to time then that is an entirely different matter. Surveys indicate that employees like to see and hear senior managers from time to time, and the messages can reinforce those in team briefing. But it is not substitute for direct, relevant dialogue between the Team Leader and the team, meeting regularly.

The Team Leader is accountable for the performance of his or her team and that is of paramount importance in connection with Team Briefing.

In a perfect world, it follows that the Chief Executive briefs the directors. They in turn brief their senior managers who go on to brief departmental heads. These people go on to brief the Team Leaders and so on.

In our imperfect world we may have a manager with, for example, four Team Leaders reporting in directly. These four are jointly responsible for only ten people. To complicate matters further, one team works a shift pattern. In these circumstances, the briefing arrangements are less obvious. Perhaps it would make more sense, and use time more effectively, if the manager were to brief the entire group of fourteen, assuming that a suitable moment could be found when they could all be together.

Alternatively, the manager might brief all four Team Leaders along with the three available teams, the shift (sub) team being briefed by their respective Team Leader while on shift.

These and other complexities are matters which must be dealt with and structured before Team Briefing is launched inside a company.

There tends to be a pay-off between two criteria when designing a team briefing structure. On the one hand the fewer levels the better, so the message has less chance of being delayed or distorted; on the other hand the teams should be as far as possible cohesive working groups.

It is vital that everyone understands the structure, which must determine who is designated to brief which team(s). In every organisation there are singletons, people working with us on a particular project, temporary staff, contractors and consultants on long term assignments. There are secretaries to consider, couriers and security staff. People on the payroll have to be briefed of course, but what of those who are with us temporarily? A decision has to be taken.

Very importantly, the usual accountability chart may differ from a Team Briefing structure chart which must be drawn up so that everyone knows who briefs whom. It may also be beneficial to draw up a separate schedule setting out information such as the location and precise time of each briefing, together with the names of designated deputy Briefers.

Successful Team Briefing arrangements begin with uncomplicated clearly defined structures.

Ultimately when something needs to be explained, people will prefer to hear it from their immediate boss. That is what should always be borne in mind.

ON A REGULAR BASIS

Planned Team Briefing on say, a monthly or bi-monthly basis will overcome the temptation to gather the team together only when it is felt there is something really earth shattering to talk about. It will also overcome the perception that meetings happen only when there is a crisis and things have 'come to a head'.

Team Briefing should ideally be linked to the moment or periods when the most up to date key performance indicators are available. In practice, most organisations review and preview activity and performance every month. Accordingly, the commencement of each briefing cycle should ideally coincide with the availability of the latest data each month.

In retail and some financial services organisations, where there is frequent product information to convey, Team Briefings often take place weekly, sometimes resulting in late opening one day a week.

It is increasingly common for Team Briefing to be combined with team meetings, which sometimes take place more frequently than monthly. In many manufacturing companies, for example, there is a 10 minute or so start of shift meeting, in some organisations concentrating on continuous improvement. Once a month, or where there is an emergency brief, the brief is attached to the beginning or end of the meeting.

The dates for Team Briefing should be published at least six months ahead. Planning them a year ahead would be even better. In this way, the time is set aside in people's diaries. Regularity suggests planning, organisation and being methodical. It also brings credibility for managers and to the process of Team Briefing.

ABOUT RELEVANT ISSUES

One of the critical factors associated with Team Briefing lies in the relevance of what is briefed. People lose interest when they can see no personal significance in what they are being told. This applies particularly to those all important global messages from the top from which people can feel remote. Getting this aspect of Team Briefing right is more important than many people realise.

In order to achieve relevancy, we have to target people with information which is directly related to what they do. Brian, in the Post Room, is unlikely to be inspired by stories about highly principled goals unless he can visualise what his contribution to them might be. The difficulty which Mary Ann is having in Procurement in acquiring reliable supplies of widgets may have absolutely no obvious implication as far as the Printing Department is concerned. Any relevance has to be clearly explained. It is as uncomplicated as that. There is no room for obscurity.

Other channels of communication should be available for background, reference or information only topics.

AN OPPORTUNITY FOR FEEDBACK

It seems difficult to envisage any briefing session during which only the voice of the Briefer is heard. In other words, where no feedback is spontaneously given or elicited. I regret to say that I have witnessed this on a number of occasions and it always seems such a pity.

Feedback is a headline word. In terms of Team Briefing it means people offering their comments, views and opinions. It manifests through questions. Getting people to 'feed back' means getting from them a reaction or response.

People want the opportunity to do so and therefore there is a facilitation issue here to consider. Team Briefing provides the opportunity for communication upwards and for this to happen at every level. It is a shame if the opportunity is squandered.

It is only in more recent years that organisations have recognised the potential of Team Briefing to elicit or solicit feedback from the process. Perhaps this evolution is attributable to the modern workforce. We are increasingly inclined to question and probe the corporate issues.

To solicit feedback also implies a degree of consultation. This can be a very healthy thing to do regarding matters which directly affect a team, for example, over the positioning of equipment, office layout, etc. It can be motivational.

THE CORE/ MANAGEMENT BRIEF

WHAT IS IT?

The Core/Management Brief is a written document, the contents of which are for dissemination to everyone in the organisation. It provides information originated at the highest level and normally deals with matters such as:

- overall financial and statistical performance

- organisational policy

- business strategy, position and adverse/favourable market influences,

- major business successes and failings

- the general direction of the business

- information about the comings and goings of the most senior people

The Core/Management Brief is usually compiled solely by the Chief Executive or collaboratively in conjunction with the directors. Very importantly, if any senior people other than the Chief are contributing to it as co-authors, this does not in any way preclude them from also preparing a Local Brief, perhaps of a divisional nature. Their 'local' input is an additional vital component.

DIRECTORATE MEETINGS

In most organisations there is a planned monthly meeting of the directors. Usually everyone in the organisation knows that these regular meetings happen. They are rarely cancelled and are seen by all as natural and very important. These are the meetings at which the major decisions are taken or rubber-stamped.

What frequently surprises staff elsewhere in the organisation is that so little of any substance seems to emerge from these senior gatherings. Team Briefing provides the formula. Additionally it can underline the importance of the issues at the top. Practice varies but usually the content of the Core/Management Brief must be briefed at every level and ultimately to everyone. It is not some sort of à la carte menu. It is regarded as sacrosanct. If we allow selectivity then clearly some people will have understanding of the more global matters and others will not. When that happens then we are back to some of the old chestnut communication problems.

If an organisation allows Briefers to be selective over Core/Management topics, then I think we might justifiably question the wisdom of having any particular point on the brief in the first place.

INTEREST LEVELS

The Core/Management Brief seems to set the tone and interest level of Team Briefing. If the information from this part of the briefing arrangement becomes regarded as dull, unimaginative or sterile then it is hardly surprising if the entire briefing process is perceived in the same humdrum way.

There are some organisations where there is no regular Core/Management Brief but where Team Briefing is nonetheless held in high regard. However, these are very rare. In an ideal world Team Briefing should be able to work effectively without a Core/Management Brief. In other words, there is adherence to the process below the level of the Chief Executive and there is no dependency upon a Core/Management Brief to make Team Briefing happen.

In my experience, people throughout any organisation might view the absence of a Core/Management Brief with suspicion. Quite apart from that, people are genuinely interested in matters at the highest level. Team Briefing is a way of raising their levels of interest and to make people feel closer to the general corporate topics. The Core/Management Brief is therefore an essential part of the process.

THE CORE/MANAGEMENT BRIEF DOCUMENT

An example of a typical, (usually A4) completed Core/Management document is shown on page 54. The information thereon tends to be little more than a bullet point summary regarding any given subject. This is good practice. If there are long and elaborate explanations then we may unwittingly encourage some merely to pass the document downwards for staff to read, or to read it out verbatim.

Succinctness and brevity are vital. So too is the need to apply some limit to the actual number of topics for dissemination. If we overload the Core/Management Brief then almost certainly some Briefers will see this as a signal that the need for their own local input is obviated. Over-focusing on the core messages can ultimately erode all local input and lead us back to the eventual lack of interest in Briefing Groups.

ACTUAL SUBSTANCE

Using the example shown, the fact that the company has won a major order with a value of £3 millions looks

Gielnick Technick

MANAGEMENT CORE BRIEF

Date brief prepared **28 September**	*Originator/s* **Louis Mann M.D.**

Note to Team Briefer

1. This brief provides the core message – add this information to your own briefing material.

2. Convey the meaning in your own words, which you know will be understood, and where possible illustrate with a practical example that is relevant to your team.

3. Words or phrases which need to convey a precise meaning will be underlined. These should not be changed in briefing.

4. Encourage questions. If you do not know the answer, say so, make a note, get the answer and give it to the questioner at the earliest possible time.

5. Ensure that you have prepared your own local brief, and have it checked by your manager, before he/she briefs you.

Subject and key points	Additional Information/Notes
PROGRESS In the face of strong competition, we have been awarded the contract to build four transmitters for LISTERS. The value of the order is £3 million. This is very good news.	More work with Listers hoped for next week.
FINANCE We are on target to end the current financial year with an operating profit of £1.1 million. In a difficult trading year this is a welcome outcome.	Our costs have been kept down. We had expected a loss of £750,000.
POLICY Following a further trial period, it has been decided to now ban smoking in all work areas. The smoking room will be refurbished shortly. Everyones co-operation is appreciated.	No plan to penalise smokers on flextime.
PEOPLE Mr Sam Gould will join the company on 1st October as Director, R & D. He will report directly to me.	Sam Gould replaces Steve O'Brien

to be good news. It does not go on to explain what this actually means to the company in detail. It does not set out divisional/departmental considerations such as material supplies, any additional necessary resourcing issues, nor the overall financial implications emanating from the order.

On the other hand, the news that the company has won such a major order might be bad news. Perhaps the company was expecting to win a substantially larger order! This is of course an extreme example but the point is an important one. As the example shows, through simple questioning more of the inside story becomes exposed and is then added by those being briefed in the space provided on the document alongside each briefing point.

This is also an example of an occasion where localisation of a 'core' message is essential. When the information is briefed to the production staff who will eventually build the transmitters, they will want a great deal more detail. Work scheduling, material specifications and resourcing are major considerations. These things may need to be briefed progressively over a number of months purely as local issues deliberately parochialised for specific teams.

The Core/Management Brief document also provides the opportunity for the author(s) to ensure that key messages are quoted verbatim if necessary. If words or sentences are underlined by the author(s) then Briefers at every level must use those words and sentences and not change or personalise them in any way. Whole tracts of the Core/Management Brief would not normally be underlined, but occasionally there may be justification for parts of it to be so.

SUMMARY

Much hinges upon the basic ability and willingness of those at the highest level to disclose topical and pertinent information for dissemination via the Core/Management Brief.

It is most unlikely that the information will always be totally scintillating. For the most part, the substance is likely to be routine.

Consistency is another key factor and there is nothing wrong in first addressing and consistently readdressing the most significant corporate issues in the Core/Management Brief. Fundamentally this should be what people expect from it.

It should also be borne in mind that the employees of any organisation would prefer not to learn about the significant goings on of the business by switching on their radio or television sets at home. It seems remarkable that the media can reveal very important news well ahead of any planned dissemination for the employees, but it happens, as many will know all too well. Some organisations have, as an explicit part of their employee communications policy, a plan to ensure that people hear first from the company.

Realistically, there are discussions at directorate level concerning all manner of things which are unworthy of any revelation to the entire workforce. There are also matters under review or consideration which eventually fizzle out and come to nothing. Add to these the inevitable business matters which will eventually find their way on to the Core/Management Brief but which are regarded as premature at a certain moment, and we have the potential for rumour mongering.

The consensus of those who have the task of preparing the Core/management Brief is that the earliest possible disclosure is a wise policy. In the context of Team Briefing, the process will be perceived as lacking credibility if matters which appear to be 'common knowledge' are not addressed. Often it is the Core/Management Brief which can and should address them.

THE LOCAL BRIEF

WHAT IS IT?

The Local Brief is also a simple written document. It is written by each line manager who is required to undertake a Team Briefing. It provides information specially aimed at particular teams. For example, in the case of an administrative support team, a Local Brief will be compiled by their immediate line boss, perhaps a Supervisor/Team Manager.

The purpose of the Local Brief is to:

- update the team regarding their performance, including comparisons

- summarise key issues relating directly to the team such as activity levels, workload, team successes, work schedules, etc

- provide a glimpse of what is expected to happen

- deal with the 'people' orientated issues, e.g. training, overtime and vacancies

- outline points for action

The Local Brief provides scope for virtually any relevant matter to be highlighted to the team and can be wide ranging. (*See Chapter 9, Subjects for Briefing*).

As with the Core/management Brief, brevity is an important factor. Long drawn out expansive explanations in very finely detailed form are unlikely to be appropriate. Indeed they are likely to induce glazed expressions.

A typical example of a completed Local Brief is shown on page 60.

McSWEENEY ENG. Corp. (HOOK)

Team Briefing

The Local Brief

Team Briefing Leader _John Duncan_ Briefing Group No __14__
Department/Section _D + E_ Date & Time of Briefing _16 April 1030am_
Names of those absent
Brian Smith
~~Peter Lyle.~~ Brief originated by _JKD_

Subjects and key points	Notes, giving examples and answers to possible questions
1. Work Progress – New Work intake for 8000 units. Overtime required to beat deadline late Sept / overall work position is favourable, up 6% on last year.	– Good NEWS. FORECAST IS ALSO UP FOR NEXT QUARTER
2. Quality All compliances met over past month No faults reported Excellent performance well done the team.	– TEAM CELEBRATION – CONFERENCE ROOM MONDAY AFTER WORK.
3. Training Training for COSMOS system begins during may. Details to follow asap.	TRAINING SKILLS INVENTORY IS BEING COMPILED. NAMES FOR TRAINING WILL FOLLOW.
4. Recruitment Recent budget approval to recruit against our vacancy for Tech. Operator. Advertising in local paper next week.	– WE HAVE HAD NO INTERNAL CANDIDATES.

continue overleaf as required

TIMING

Each leader must prepare a Local Brief **in advance** of the briefing cycle dates.

Once the briefing cycle dates have been established and published, everyone who has a briefing role will know well in advance precisely when he/she must prepare the Local Brief.

For some, this is an ongoing task. As any month progresses and issues crop up which the whole team should be aware of, line Briefers make notes and store them in a file ready to be briefed. Other Briefers are more inclined to gather data nearer to the actual date when they are to give the briefing.

In the case of an organisation in which the Core/Management Brief begins its cascade on, say, the second Tuesday of each month and the briefing cycle is designated as being three days in duration, each Briefer will know the moment when he or she is to be briefed and when he or she is to undertake his or her own. It is a question of having these 'windows' scheduled well in advance both upwards and downwards within the cycle.

A word of caution: obviously you should not store up important matters which need to be explained or dealt with outside the briefing cycle. Team Briefing should not be a substitute for day-to-day dialogue between the leader and the team. It is far better if Team Briefing is regarded as a consolidated review and preview session.

FAILURE

Team Briefing can falter or be far less effective if any individual line Briefer fails to compile a Local Brief for each briefing cycle. It is the most common reason given by staff for Team Briefing to sometimes be regarded as lacking interest. It also deprives peers of the sharing opportunity within the drill.

Amongst the excuses given for Briefers not preparing a Local Brief are:

> 'I couldn't think of anything worth saying.' (!)
> 'They know it already.' (!)
> 'I couldn't get ten minutes to myself.'
> 'My people aren't really interested.' (!)
> 'There's nothing new to say.'
> 'It's all in my boss's brief.'
> 'My nerves got the better of me.'
> 'There's nothing much happening at the moment.'
> 'I've got toothache at the moment.'
> 'I've forgotten what I have to do.'
> 'I meant to do it but the Football Pools lady called.'

The full list reads like that of some of the more bizarre, imaginative reasons people give for being late for work/school. They never seem valid when closely scrutinised.

Training people so that they fully understand their roles in briefing is absolutely essential. When doing so, particular attention should be paid to the preparation of the Local Brief. It is one of the critical factors affecting any Team Briefing process.

If, following training, first line leaders are still having difficulty thinking of topics, the frequency of the meeting may not be appropriate. Paradoxically, it is easier for first line leaders to think of things to say daily than monthly, since the working cycle is more likely to be daily or weekly than monthly.

NEWSCASTING

There are three other points to consider.

Typically, during any routine Team Briefing, most questioning and feedback from the team will be in connection with the local matters. Without a Local Brief, there will be far less feedback.

People are naturally interested in the bigger picture, but they are also concerned with local matters. It is these which are far more likely to directly affect them and therefore involve them.

Let's hope that the day never comes when the TV local newscaster opens with the words, 'There is nothing worth telling you today, . . . nothing has really happened and nothing is expected to happen tomorrow. However, we hope you enjoyed the national news piece regarding the UK's export of live snails to France. Wasn't it interesting?'

Relating this to Team Briefing, you can see just how the absence of a manager's Local Brief can appear from the perspective of the team. Extraordinary seems to be an appropriate word. There is *always* something happening and something will be happening tomorrow.

AND FINALLY . . .

The ratio of information from the Core/Management Brief and that from Local Briefs is important. A good ratio at the base line team level is approximately 30% from the Core/Management and Directors' Briefs and 70% from the combined Local Briefs.

This is not an absolutely critical factor but if the balance ever goes too far in favour of the Core/Management Brief messages, then it will be to the detriment of localisation. That could cause an over focus upon the 'big' messages which are not always seen as relevant.

The diagram on page 64 highlights this point.

The Brief 'cake'

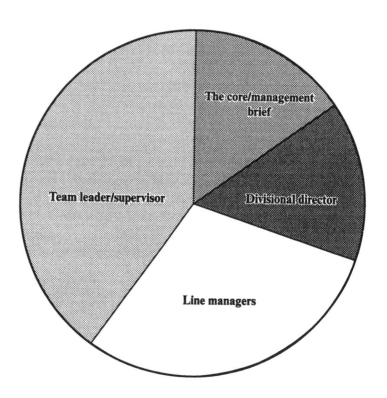

FEEDBACK

WHAT IS IT?

Communication is not a one way process. Whatever we read or hear we have a brain response. That response might cause a number of reactions. It could be that through our reaction we are stirred into action, we say or do something – or not; maybe understanding has been created – or not.

Feedback manifests itself through comment and through people otherwise expressing themselves. This could be through people stating their views, opinions, concerns or their ideas.

It might also be a straightforward QUESTION but equally perhaps a case of non-oral expression or body language.

In Team Briefing today, feedback in relation to what is being briefed is both expected and encouraged. Whereas with Briefing Groups little or no feedback was forthcoming nor elicited, modern Team Briefing has evolved more towards a two way process.

Team Briefing is essentially a system for providing management information. It is about dissemination, and it is principally a telling arrangement. So, to promote Team Briefing as a perfectly balanced two-way communication process is inappropriate, because it has no equilibrium.

An effort should be made, however, to elicit as much feedback as possible.

QUESTIONS

Having made these points, Team Briefing should encourage people to vocalise their thoughts and to ask questions. Questions and answers create understanding, not only for the questioner, but for everyone else listening.

It is entirely natural for people to be inquisitive and to probe beyond the headlines, especially in connection with the all important 'Why?' factors.

Briefers at every level will feel the need to question and will want to feed back in some way to their senior Briefer during the briefing session. In doing so they will hopefully fully understand the implications and the inside story relating to any given topic which they must subsequently brief onwards.

Team members will also wish to feed back. Whilst comments, views and opinions can be expected from time to time, for the most part their feedback will be in the form of a direct question aimed at their Briefer. Logically, if we declare to the teams that feedback is regarded as an essential and integral aspect of Team Briefing, then clearly we should manage it, and be seen to manage it effectively.

ANSWERS

Providing answers to questions is therefore a fundamental part of the Team Briefing process. In most organisations there is scope to obtain answers to a wide range of sometimes perceptive and imaginative questions.

The key points for Briefers are:

- Questions should not be ducked nor disallowed.

- Equivocation and prevarication should be avoided.

- If a Briefer knows the answer, it should be provided, clearly and succinctly. It should not be referred upwards unnecessarily.

- Guessing at answers is a mistake. Even if Briefers say something like, '. . . well, I'm not really sure but I would imagine that . . .,' this will induce even more searching questioning.

- If Briefers do not know the answer to a question they should simply SAY SO. This should be followed by an offer to refer the question (upwards if necessary), and for the answer to be provided as soon as possible.

- Answers to 'referred' questions should be provided by the teams' Briefer within a few working days.

- It is the responsibility of Briefers themselves to ensure that a 'referred' question is dealt with expediently and subsequently provided to the questioner. There is no communication equivalent of the tooth fairy.

- Briefers should bear in mind that if there are long delays in providing answers to 'referred' questions, the value of Team Briefing itself will be questioned. It will also perhaps provoke irascibility.

- It is usually unnecessary to call the team together again simply for them to hear the answer to a 'referred' question. However, the cynics and pessimists in any team will be carefully noting whether or not any outstanding question has been dealt with. It is therefore sensible subsequently to inform the entire team who heard such a question being asked, that the question was satisfactorily answered. This might be done at the next briefing.

- Staff should not always expect to receive written answers to questions, although in some cases it may be appropriate.

THE FEEDBACK LOOP

Recording outfall on to a Feedback Form has become standard practice in many organisations. Any belief that this is unnecessarily bureaucratic can be easily dispelled when the advantages are considered.

The advantages are that:

- It provides proof that the Team Briefing has actually taken place.

- The form can be used as a vehicle to deal with questions which have to be referred.

- It can be a focus for one-to-one discussions between a Briefer and his/her line manager.

- Through a co-ordinated 'loop', individual briefing matters may be recycled and readdressed. It also becomes possible to identify common reactions throughout a workforce.

- Particular issues raised at any particular Team Briefing can be spotlighted and, if relevant, drawn to the attention of other teams or parts of the organisation.

The only disadvantage of using a Feedback Form is that Briefers actually have to write them up. However, this is one of those five minute tasks which can be so beneficial.

The two examples shown on pages 71–72 are fairly typical. Organisations might prefer to design their own forms depending upon what they want specifically from the arrangement.

Each Briefer is required to complete a Feedback Form immediately following the briefing session. In some cases they can ask one of the team members to note questions or other feedback during the meeting. A copy of the form should be retained by the Briefer. Two additional copies are required, one for the Briefer's line manager and one for the Team Briefing Co-ordinator. (*See* Chapter 11, The Co-ordinator)

Sometimes when particular points are briefed, they may create an unanticipated reaction and the need for greater clarity becomes apparent. Through the Co-ordinator examining the Feedback Forms, it becomes possible to readdress them during the next briefing cycle. If urgent clarification is necessary then obviously it would be unwise to wait another month before providing it.

SPECIAL TEAM BRIEFINGS

In many companies 'special' Team Briefings are called from time to time outside the usual briefing cycle. These can be convened to deal with major matters which crop up, such as, for example, in connection with a major order that has been won. In the same way special briefings can be used to deal with the outfall from a briefing cycle. The need for them is rare but once the Team Briefing formula is established, non-cyclical briefings can also become a bonus of the process.

THE CO-ORDINATOR AND FEEDBACK

The Co-ordinator may have an important role in relation to the feedback arrangements. Quite apart from acting as a monitor of the process as a whole the Co-ordinator could also:

- Provide a detailed summary of the feedback from any cycle directly to the Chief Executive. In doing so, upwards filtering through the layers is avoided.

- Check that answers to referred questions are dealt with quickly and expediently.

- Publish a monthly/quarterly summary of the more interesting questions and answers highlighted through the feedback loop.

Whilst some or all of these arrangements for managing feedback may be very beneficial, we should keep a sense of proportion. Realistically, approximately 95% of all questions raised at any Team Briefing session are successfully dealt with at the time. The need for referral is minimal.

A proceduralised feedback arrangement will primarily bring benefit through the line management layers. By completing a Feedback Form after each briefing, and sending a copy upwards, Briefers highlight their teams' reactions to the briefing topics, and some of these are likely to be significant at certain times.

One-to-one dialogue between the Briefer and his/her line manager regarding Team Briefing is good management practice. The Feedback Form can help this happen.

Two final points regarding feedback. It should not be the responsibility of a Team Briefing Co-ordinator to deal with referred questions. In organisations where this arrangement has been practised, it fails to work well. It is important to manage this through the line. Secondly, Briefers find that because most questioning/feedback from their team concerns local issues, careful preparation of the Local Brief is a major success factor. When preparing this, likely questions can be anticipated and the need for referral kept to a minimum.

LESSEY MARKETING (HIGH WYCOMBE)

FEEDBACK FORM

Briefing Team	6 (LRD)	*Team Briefer*	VAL TYLER
Date of Briefing	14 NOVEMBER	*Time*	2·00 p.m.

List of questions outstanding from last month NONE

Three dealt with during past month

List of unanswered questions

Is there any plan to operate a week-end shift for the Help Desk? Systems and Programme support is becoming increasingly necessary.

REMEMBER IT IS YOUR RESPONSIBILITY TO FIND OUT AND REPORT BACK ANSWERS TO THESE QUESTIONS

QUESTIONS SHOULD BE ANSWERED WITHIN 5 WORKING DAYS OF THE BRIEFING

Brief note on questions asked

Plans to reduce current workload.
Also questions regarding Admin Support & Office reorganisation.

What was of most interest to your team?

Consultations over Performance Related Pay.
More news a.s.a.p. please.

Positive suggestions made

Various feasible ideas regarding forthcoming office moves All dealt with.

Copies to be sent to i) Review Group (via) and ii) Immediate Manager.
Original copy to be returned by Team Briefer.

VRT. 14/11

FEEDBACK FORM

TEAM NUMBER 6	NAME OF BRIEFER Adamford
DATE OF BRIEF 14 April	LOCATION COUSAC

1. HOW DID YOUR TEAM BRIEFING GO? Significant comments in relation to Project Alice and impact upon generation levels.

2. KEY QUESTIONS RAISED BY YOUR TEAM	ANSWER GIVEN (IF ANSWER REFERRED UPWARDS WRITE 'REFERRED UP')
a) Overtime issues b) Safety procedures c) Target setting d) Project overrun	Will the new staff be trained here or at Petersdown? "Referred up"

REMEMBER! - GET ANSWERS FOR OUTSTANDING QUESTIONS TO ENQUIRIES WITHIN 48 HOURS IF POSSIBLE.

3. WHAT WERE THE PRINCIPAL ITEMS YOU ADDED TO THE REGIONAL CORE AND DISTRICT LOCAL BRIEFS.

(a) Work in progress
(b) Priority workloads
(c) TQ initiative — BSEN ISO 9001
(d)
(e) Training

4. ANY OTHER MAJOR POINTS ARISING FROM YOUR BRIEF-. Significant interest in departmental reorganisation

● WHAT WAS OF MOST INTEREST TO YOUR TEAM?

Project Alice - again

● POSITIVE/CONSTRUCTIVE SUGGESTIONS MADE?

Detailed training plans for next Team Briefing

NOW SEND A COPY OF THIS FORM TO YOUR BOSS AND THE TEAM BRIEFING CO-ORDINATORS. ANSWERS TO QUESTIONS ARE THE RESPONSIBILITY OF THE LINE MANGERS.

THE DRILL

OUTLINE

At the heart of every successful Team Briefing process is conformity to a straightforward drill. The specific arrangements to operate the drill will vary from company to company according to the briefing structure. However, it is always based upon five stages.

These are:

- **Prepare your local brief.**
- **Attend the briefing of your line manager and have your brief checked and shared.**
- **Hear your line managers briefing.**
- **Ask questions, feedback, clarify and probe.**
- **Subsequently, brief your team.**

This sequence of activity is essential if we are to ensure Briefers at all levels understand the issues to be briefed before undertaking briefing further down.

PREPARING YOUR OWN BRIEF

Team Briefing is weakened if any line manager fails to prepare a brief. Preparing a brief is a simple matter but it seems to cause consternation in the minds of some. This matter is analysed in Chapters 6 and 9.

ATTEND YOUR BOSS'S BRIEFING

Few Briefers have a one-to-one briefing from their line manager. For most Briefers this is a peer group briefing, the timing for which is set to synchronise with the arrangements within each cycle of briefing further up the chain.

For example, four line managers within a Marketing Department will together attend the briefing of their General Manager of Marketing Division. It is their natural affinity group and it is this primary factor which normally governs the whole matter of who briefs whom. In management briefings, there is often a regular management meeting anyway, in which team briefing can feature on the agenda.

PEER GROUP BRIEFINGS

At the briefing session several matters have to be dealt with.

First, each line manager in turn is required to outline the substance of his or her Local Brief orally. These are issues of direct relevance to each of the line managers' briefing teams.

Vitally the senior manager 'chairing' the briefing will then therefore know in advance what matters are being disseminated within the function for which he or she is accountable. This is another major bonus of Team Briefing.

SHARING INFORMATION

A consequence of each line manager vocalising the substance of his or her Local Brief is that the opportunity then exists for a fundamental sharing of information within a peer group. The Advertising Manager will hear what the Marketing Policy Manager is going to brief to the Marketing Policy team and vice versa.

In doing so, each manager may learn of something which is of relevance or has some significance to the other peer group teams. In other words, they can pick up snippets of news from each other. This process may be orchestrated by the 'chairperson' who may direct or suggest to the line managers (Briefers) that they might add the additional information to their Local Briefs. Alternatively, Briefers add things they pick up in a less formal way, knowing whether or not something which a peer is saying is relevant to their team.

It is impossible to overstate the importance of this sharing process. Team Briefing is a line management function and it is not necessarily designed to deal with cross functional matters. However, it can deal with what are regarded as the co-lateral issues: but only if every single Briefer prepares a Local Brief in the first place.

PAPER COPIES

The 'chairperson' will then brief the four line managers. He or she will provide a paper copy of his/her own Local (Divisional) Brief, as well as a copy of the Core/Management Brief. Both have to be explained (briefed) orally.

As each item is explained it is important that the opportunity is provided for feedback. Additional information is perhaps elicited in this way which has to be recorded on to the appropriate briefing documents. Part of the objective here is to also look for local angles in relation to the global messages, and to predict questions.

At every briefing after that of the most senior managers, each Briefer is required to hand on copies of the briefing documents and complete a Feedback Form. It is the responsibility of the 'chairperson' to ensure that briefees provide feedback, and to check for misunderstanding.

The final step of the drill is for the managers who have now been briefed to undertake briefing to the next level below.

If the team includes Briefers, then they too will have prepared a Local Brief in advance of being briefed. The drill is applied at every level involving Briefers. It is only at the final level, that there is no need of the sharing drill. Nor is there a need to provide each and every team member with a copy of the briefing documents.

TIMING AND SPEED

It is sensible to build into the drill some time lapses. If Briefers emerge from their upward briefing, and immediately dash off to brief their teams, then they have had insufficient time to review the issues and prioritise them.

It is imperative that there should not be unnecessary verbatim reading from the briefing documents. Far better to use your own language when giving the background to any issue. Briefers who allow themselves time to give thought to this important aspect of the process will invariably be more successful than those who rely on last minute ad-libbing.

If, for example, a Briefer attends his boss's briefing during the morning, then he/she should aim to brief the team(s) during the afternoon or even perhaps on the following working day. In this way, the briefing points will have been digested, mulled over and prioritised. The time lapse also provides more time for possible questions from the team to be anticipated. If the Briefer is anticipating in this way then there is far more likelihood that questions will be answered successfully.

It is true that what is being advocated here will prolong and protract a briefing cycle. However, the potential gain in effectiveness outweighs the disadvantage of perhaps adding a day to the overall briefing cycle. In any case, the speed of dissemination is not a primary consideration. Doing the job well is.

It is important, too, where possible, to have the final briefs happening simultaneously in all departments. This prevents people from hearing most of the items from their friends before they are briefed.

SUBJECTS FOR BRIEFING

BACKGROUND

A great deal depends upon the ability and willingness of Briefers at every level to highlight matters of substance and importance through the Team Briefing process.

The need for disclosure, openness and honesty is probably obvious but it is also paramount. Team Briefing can become tarnished if the subject matter becomes in any way perceived as insipid, innocuous or inert. This can also be the case if it is used only to convey good news when people in the organisation know that there is much bad news lurking. The reverse is also true.

If we were to take a snapshot of any organisation today, we would actually see that there are both good and not so good stories which could be disseminated. Any exaggeration of either, provides an unbalanced impression of the true picture. Reflecting the balance is a vital key. So too is the simple requirement to address the subjects which interest people. In general these are the subjects which drive the business and are relatively easy to identify. Making these subjects matter to people is largely a question of how well we convey them.

Team Briefing can be an enlightening experience for everyone but equally it can be most unenlightening. It can have a low profile or a high one. Team Briefing can and should create understanding, but it might not. If it is undertaken in a well managed way then there are significant benefits to be gained. If it isn't, then we may expect very little in return for our efforts and time.

In the organisations where Team Briefing has a high profile and is highly regarded, we inevitably find that one of the principal reasons for its success lies in the actual subject matter being briefed.

THE GOOD NEWS

People today have to work hard. The demands upon individuals are substantial and many work long hours, often without extra pay. Former days of over manning and demarcation seem to have gone for ever.

In consequence, there is more pressure and even stress in the workplace. Each time a vacancy is deliberately left unfilled it is almost certain this will result in extra work for someone, perhaps for a whole team, as they absorb the additional tasks.

People give a great deal of themselves to bring about success and when such success has been achieved it is usually a relief, a cause to celebrate and something to crow about.

If we set people targets and quotas, and then constantly evaluate what is being accomplished, we will know when something has been achieved. Achievement is a major motivating factor. It applies at every level within an organisation. It could be associated with winning a huge export order or something as basic as completing an important piece of work on time.

Whatever it is, it is worthy of praise for those involved. Achievement is invariably brought about by teamwork and it means a great deal to people.

Team Briefing is a perfect medium for talking about our successes and for appropriate levels of praise.

THE NOT SO GOOD NEWS

This is not a euphemism. There is a vast difference between bad news and news which is not so good as it could be. Differentiating between the two when talking to people can do much to create understanding and avoid misunderstanding.

Bad news suggests failure and may be regarded as threatening. This may well be the case but whatever it is it needs to be put into perspective. Addressing and explaining bad news early on can cause less anxiety in the longer term.

Converting bad news and problems into language which people can understand and telling them what they mean are essential.

Without unambiguous clarification people could mistakenly believe that all is lost when it probably isn't. Nothing can be more thoroughly demoralising. If things are bad, what is being done to bring about improvement? Presumably something. And what will be the likely effect on the teams?

The same applies to the not so good news. Frankness mixed with a degree or two of empathy will be appreciated far more than statements designed to pull the wool over people's eyes.

Team Briefing is a means of keeping people up to date. Using it in a pre-emptive way to suddenly disclose major corporate trauma is rarely the wisest thing to do. On the other hand, providing meaningful progress reports is good management practice, so that if bad news comes, it is not such a shocking surprise.

THE FOUR P'S

For many years The Industrial Society has suggested classifying briefing topics under four main headings, which many find useful.

PROGRESS

POLICY

PEOPLE

POINTS FOR ACTION

There is scope for four more headings.

PLANS

PRAISE

PRIORITIES

PROCEDURES

Examples of the four P's are given on page 84. These are the sorts of topics which people like to hear about. There are many more.

It seems fortuitous that all eight main subject headings begin with the letter 'P'. That should make them easy to remember. However, some brief expansion of the four additional headings is called for.

PLANS

There are major corporate plans, business plans, divisional and departmental plans. There are plans to change, develop, modify and improve. Planning is a primary business imperative and it shapes organisations for the future. More than any other topic people want to know what is being planned and why.

Planning is futuristic, which is why people are always interested.

PRAISE

A simple statement of thanks for a good team performance can have a motivational effect. The ongoing absence of it can have the opposite effect.

It seems that we are quick to point out shortcomings and individual mistakes but slow to tell people when things are going well. This creates sourness.

A middle manager in Production once told me that his job was to police the production area looking out for shortcomings. When he discovered one, he had to put things right and find the culprit(s). He added that this was a pity because 99.9% of the time his people did a first class job. So it was more a case for praise, but that was not part of his policing role, he said.

Excessive praise is often regarded as patronising in some way, so getting the amount of appropriate praise right is vital. Getting the specifics right is important too. Broad praise for the entire workforce will not mean very much unless we point out what a particular team's achievement was.

Team briefing: Examples of subjects

These subjects have been briefed in various organisations. You may choose to use some of them or think up your own subjects. They have been grouped under the "4P's": People, Progress, Policy, Points for action.

PROGRESS
Product sales
Market share
Planning
Trading Position
Development of subsidiaries
Financial results
Contracts gained/lost
Circulation figures
Cost comparisons
Export sales
Competitors products
Quality index
Waste reduction
Safety comparisons
Productivity figures
Safe driving awards
Faults
Key depressions
Budgets
Sales targets
Accident record
Order position
Company achievement
New products

PEOPLE
Appointments
Resignations
Promotions
Internal vacancies
Selection procedure
Relocation of personnel
Overtime levels
Time-keeping
Company visits
Customer visits
Absenteeism
Long service awards
Labour turnover
Grievance/disciplinary procedures
Training courses attendance
Job security
Attendance at union branch meetings
Research into selection
Management development programs
Conference plans

POLICY
Team briefing/communication
Legislation
Change in procedures
Supervisor development programme
Expansion plans
Capital investment programme
New committees formed
Advertising policy
Employee share purchase plan
Setting up of new division
Industrial relations statement
Factory re-organisation/extension plans
Job evaluation exercise
Employees savings scheme
Drivers insurance
Suppliers hold ups
Short time working
New product information
Project reports
Long/short term company objectives
Training courses
Pension courses
Canteen changes
Energy saving campaign

POINTS FOR ACTION
Explanations of efficiency monitoring system
Fulfilling orders quickly
Sub-contractors on site
Emergency procedures
Suggestion scheme
Heating, ventilation system
Accident reporting
Fire prevention
Start up after annual break
Stock shrinkage
Private phone calls
Car parking
Dealing with VAT
Production of invoices
Maintenance priorities
Materials shortage
Increased costs
Stock discrepancies
Shortage of raw materals
Dealing with complaints
Non-decisions
Correcting of 'grapevine' rumours
Security
Safeguarding of confidential information
Quality
Safety
Housekeeping campaign

PRIORITIES

In management we are sometimes seen to change priorities. This is almost certainly a good thing. It indicates that we are being watchful and adjusting according to the day-to-day needs of the business.

The complaint however is that people fail to understand why, yesterday, job or project 'A' had a higher priority than job or project 'B', and today that's all changed.

It's a simple matter of WIIY. That is what people want to hear. It is also a question of management credibility. Rather than have people telling one another that the management don't seem to know what they are doing, we could claim credit for adjusting priorities for both timely and objective reasons. Acquainting people with management rationale is a healthy prerequisite to gaining commitment.

PROCEDURES

Procedures are the routines which govern our working lives. They determine the steps and processes which are designed to get the job done. Procedures have to be adjusted from time to time to maximise efficiency and customer satisfaction.

Team Briefing offers an ideal opportunity to explain changes to working practices and their effect on teams. It can also give team members the opportunity to feed back any improvements generated from procedural revisions or explain any unforeseen snags.

QUALITY

Quality Improvement is related to this. The drive for ever higher quality standards through continuous improvement is arguably one of the best things to ever happen to world trade. Running businesses to meet customer expectation and always exploring better ways of doing things has transformed organisations.

In many there are compliance and conformance standards and a host of Quality Management Systems. Spotlighting key quality issues through Team Briefing can retain ongoing focus on Quality.

MENTAL CHECKLIST

Effective Briefers prepare well. They do so as each month progresses, making notes about things they need to raise at the next Team Briefing session.

Leaving the preparation until the last possible moment can be unwise. TO FAIL TO PREPARE IS TO PREPARE TO FAIL. How true in relation to Team Briefing.

Having made these points, a simple checklist (in addition to the 'P' headings) used sensibly either during the course of each month, or nearer the day of briefing, may be helpful.

Briefers should ask themselves some questions, such as:

- What problems exist? What is being done about them, when will they go away, if not, why not, and what effects are the problems having on the business and the team?

- What improvements are necessary, specifically?

- What are we aiming at?

- What's expected to happen?

- What deadlines exist?

- What successes have there been?

- What's changing and why?

- Who's doing anything special?

- How do we compare?

- What's on the grapevine?

- Are we doing all we can?

For very many years, The Industrial Society has expressed effective leadership through the Action Centred Leadership model. It is based upon three interlocked circles.

The three distinct issues, task, team and individual, are inexorably inter-related. Bearing this in mind when constructing a brief will help to shape it.

SUMMARY

Preparing a Local Brief each month should not be an ordeal. In this chapter I have tried to point out that there is an extremely wide ranging menu of topics which could be relevant to any team.

The problem should be one of careful selection from the menu and what to leave out. It should never be one of having nothing worth saying.

Two final summary points regarding preparation of the brief.

1) Preparing your brief in advance is a fundamental requirement of the drill. Without it a Briefer is depriving his or her peers of the opportunity to share the local matters concerning another team. Briefers who prepare their Local Brief **after** having been briefed, and it has to be said that some do so, are far less likely to be effective as Briefers. They have a tendency to waste time trying to localise the topics from the Core/Management Brief, or from the Brief provided by their senior Briefer. This is not always possible. As a consequence, their teams will invariably miss out on a purely Local Brief aimed specifically at them. Proactivity is the key to successful Local Briefing.

2) Briefers who prepare at least the bones of a Local Brief during the course of a month are far more likely to present their local information in a positive way. Consequently, they are less likely to induce the negative reactions which can undermine both Team Briefing and management credibility.

It is as profoundly important as that.

GIVING A BRIEFING

BACKGROUND

Team Briefing does not involve giving a presentation, nor does it involve giving a speech. Team Briefing requires the Briefers of any organisation to TALK to their teams and to explain what is happening and why.

This is not a particularly difficult thing to do. But to gain proficiency and maximise the true potential of Team Briefing, there are skills which can be learned and developed.

In this book I have tried to explain the rationale and structures of Team Briefing. I have also examined some of the logistics and good practices in successfully operating it. I have intentionally not elaborated the individual delivery skills element of the process.

Oral delivery in Team Briefing is an important separate subject. There is a vast array of additional information and advice which could be provided. However, it is absolutely essential that everyone who is a designated Briefer is provided with at least one day's training before they have to brief.

It is wrong to assume that leaders can spontaneously undertake Team Briefing without it. The process will never get off the ground without effective training.

Briefers need fully to understand the mechanisms of the process and how everything fits together. Each individual Briefer's part in operating Team Briefing is crucial in making it work effectively. Briefers need to understand this.

SPECIFIC NEEDS

The Team Briefing training must also be designed to take account of the particular needs of individuals. Briefers in first line management roles such as supervisors or team leaders will probably need more help with delivery skills than those in senior management, but this cannot be assumed.

An overriding objective should be that Team Briefing gets management information across to the teams in a professional way. It would be a pity if, when all the drills and disciplines are working well and the briefing subject matter is truly interesting and topical, Briefers then convey it to people in a boring and lacklustre way by simply quoting directly from the briefing documents.

Team Briefing does not require Briefers to be slick, highly polished television type newscasters. Equally, we need to avoid the '. . . it says here' or '. . . I've been asked to tell you' extremes.

Training is the key to success and organisations will probably benefit a great deal from calling in professional help to get the process absolutely right and to address specific training needs. Those needs are likely to be different in every organisation and tailoring the training accordingly is important.

In fact, it is sometimes worth delaying skills training until AFTER the Briefers have done it two or three times. By then, Briefers themselves will have learned more or less what it might take to deliver information face-to-face and of any personal shortcomings. Their input into developing appropriate skills training packages would help to avoid the sheep dip approach which might otherwise occur.

YOU CAN'T NOT COMMUNICATE

Research proves that when someone gives a spoken message, the listeners' understanding and judgement of that message comes from:

7% WORDS	Words are labels and listeners can put their own interpretations on them.
38% PARALINGUISTIC	The WAY in which something is said (i.e. accent, tone, inflection etc.) is very important to a listener's understanding.
55% FACIAL EXPRESSIONS	What a speaker looks like while delivering a message affects the listener's understanding most of all.

(Research Source – Albert Mehrabian)

This supports the belief that if Briefers merely speak face down while reading information from a script (the briefing documents), then they may not create the understanding.

PREPARATION

Effective Team Briefers prepare notes for themselves, usually written in bullet point form and merely glance at them during the course of a briefing. They use face contact to get the points across rather than present to the group only the tops of their heads. And they use their own words to convey the meaning of the written words and not those of someone else.

Beyond this there are additional general points to bear in mind.

Briefers should:

USE EXAMPLES	To illustrate the topics.
PLAN WHAT HAS TO BE SAID	Not only what but in what sequence. The most important information first. (Not always the Core/Management information)
ANTICIPATE QUESTIONS	Some will be obvious and others less so. Successful answering creates the 'feel good factor' for everyone.
ANTICIPATE DISTRACTIONS	For example, avoiding excessive noise and diverting phone calls away from the briefing area are obvious things to be done.
AVOID EMBELLISHMENT	Clear, concise statements are preferable. Rambling explanations are unnecessary.
USE VISUAL AIDS	A picture is worth a thousand words. Simple graphs or drawings will

aid understanding. This is especially important in presenting financial or other performance information.

ENCOURAGE FEEDBACK

By pausing every now and again and inviting feedback. This is infinitely better than hurrying along to get it over with. Soliciting feedback is often necessary.

Above all else, Briefers need to understand how to conduct themselves when briefing. Those who expect to fail will fail. It's a self fulfilling prophesy. Their performance has to be checked and monitored over time. It is all part of managing communications.

These are just a few good practice guidelines. There are many more which may need to be taken into account when planning a company's Team Briefing process or in revitalising an existing one.

SUMMARY

It is worth remembering that Briefers who appear to undertake their Team Briefings in unflustered way are almost certainly employing simple techniques. They will be well prepared and regard Team Briefing not as a monthly chore, but as part of being a manager. It is, after all essentially a leadership issue.

TRAINING FOR TEAM BRIEFING

WHAT'S INVOLVED?

There are six primary training considerations:

- Awareness Training
- Training Briefers
- The Co-ordinator
- Skills Training
- Long Term Training
- Ongoing Coaching

As with any form of training, it has to be structured, planned, designed and fit for purpose. Training people in relation to the principles, management and skills of Team Briefing is profoundly important and should not be underestimated or skimped.

A problem associated with training is that it is sometimes regarded as remedial. Some actually resent devoting time to being in a training room, especially experienced managers who perhaps feel that they have seen it all before. Worse, they can perceive training rooms as correction centres where underperformers are sent as a last resort. As a consequence, there can be resistance to training and this has to be dealt with.

Another potential problem is some people's belief that the introduction of Team Briefing is little more than a new 'flavour of the month' thing to do. It can be seen as a passing fad and the cynics and sceptics will need convincing that it is not.

They will perhaps claim that they are already communicating effectively with their staff and this may well be the case. Team Briefing is a company-wide initiative and its introduction should never be viewed as a criticism of individuals.

COMMITMENT

The first pre-requisite in establishing effective Team Briefing lies in commitment 'from the top'. The second pre-requisite also lies in commitment 'from the top'.

The need for commitment at the highest levels cannot be over stated. It is a crucial factor. Middle and junior managers tend to adopt the values of their seniors. It is therefore very damaging if, for example, a director appears to support Team Briefing in the presence of his or her peers, but who quietly confides to others that this is not actually so. The word will quickly go around and adversely influence other Briefers.

There is a need to ensure that there is commitment to Team Briefing at all levels. Training can play an important part in achieving this.

Commitment is intangible. We are more likely to assess someone's commitment by what they do rather than what they say.

Therefore, tangible actions are needed in addition to assertions if Team Briefing is to flourish. The Chief Executive and the senior management team must be seen actively to support Team Briefing through their actions. Training is one of the important actions because it creates understanding.

AWARENESS TRAINING

Very often an important first step is for someone who understands the finer points of Team Briefing to provide an overview to the senior management team.

A ninety minute presentation which allows for questions and answers will do nothing but good. Any anxieties, misgivings or misconceptions can be addressed within the senior peer group itself, and will not therefore spill over to the other levels of management perhaps in a training room.

There may also be a strong case in favour of providing an overview of Team Briefing to the entire workforce. If so, it is more likely to be successful if it is done in small groups or aimed at the actual work teams.

If unions are recognised then it is both courteous and sound management practice to explain Team Briefing to the representatives. They will be briefed in their respective teams but they will appreciate a separate Awareness session.

The provision of Awareness Training simply needs to be thought through and built into a timetable of activity (Implementation Plan), leading up to a pre-determined implementation date. An example of this is shown on page 98.

TRAINING BRIEFERS

Everyone who is designated as a Briefer must be trained. This includes senior management team members and also anyone who is to be a deputy Briefer.

The duration of training will vary but one full day should be regarded as a minimum.

Essential minimum in-house training modules are:

- **the reasons why Team Briefing is being introduced: for example, communication problems, Quality compliance, staff involvement policy, Investors in People initiative etc**

- **the need for regular, well structured meetings**

PROJECT IMPLEMENTATION CHART

ACTION/STAGES	CALENDER - WEEK ENDING														ACTION BY
	2.7	9.7	16.7	23.7	30.7	6.8	13.8	20.8	27.8	6.9	13.9	20.9	27.9	4.10	
Presentations to Senior Management Team	▓														
Draw up Structure Chart and Schedules		▓													
Design Paperwork and Customise Binders			▓	▓											
Design and agree Training Plans					▓	▓									
Allocate Briefers to Training Courses															
Final Approval for Training Plans								▓							
Training for Briefers Head Office										▓	▓				
Training for Briefers Regional Offices												▓	▓		
Evaluation of Training Feedback													▓	▓	

- the value of communication as part of leadership

- what Team Briefing is – The Drill

- the Core/Management and Local Brief

- what to brief, relevance

- understanding and managing feedback

- briefing skills

- management communication policy and standards of performance

- the role of the Co-ordinator

- monitoring arrangements

Additional modules will probably be required, supported by videofilm, appropriate documentation and examples.

At each training course, Briefers should practise preparing a Local Brief and undertake briefing in small groups using The Drill. A sample Core/Management brief will be needed in order to bring this component of the process to life.

Serious consideration should be given to bringing in outside training professionals to provide this training. Team Briefing is a very specialist subject and training for it has to be absolutely right and well structured.

THE CO-ORDINATOR

By appointing a Co-ordinator for Team Briefing very early on, the training logistics and arrangements can be identified and managed through the Co-ordinator channel. In large organisations this can be a major operation.

The Co-ordinator should also attend the same training programme as that provided for Briefers to ensure understanding of what the process involves.

Later on, once Team Briefing is established, the Co-ordinator could input directly at future training courses aimed at newly appointed leaders. Training for new Briefers should be planned for, perhaps through the Co-ordinator, and could include a module highlighting his or her role.

SKILLS TRAINING

Delivery skills, questioning and listening skills all have a potential place within training courses for Team Briefing, but they are optional modules.

When designing Team Briefing training, it is important to make a judgement about the very specific training needs of individuals, over and above the minimum requirements.

LONG TERM TRAINING

Provision should be made for newly appointed leaders to be trained in connection with Team Briefing. Some means of ensuring that the names of these people are always automatically fed through to the Co-ordinator needs to be established.

Whether it is possible to train new leaders through internal means, or perhaps send them to attend Team Briefing training externally, should be determined in advance.

Essentially, no one should be expected to undertake Team Briefing without first having been trained to do so.

ONGOING COACHING

Through effective monitoring, including one-to-one dialogue between more senior managers and their subordinate Briefers, it becomes possible to provide additional help for those who may need it.

This is almost certainly something which can be dealt with through the line management chain, rather than through seeking more formal training solutions. In fact it is preferable to do so. Alternatively, the Co-ordinator may be able to provide additional guidance to individuals.

Coaching individual Briefers to achieve higher standards is good management practice. It is objective both in terms of improved performance but also because it demonstrates commitment to the process by more senior management.

MONITORING TEAM BRIEFING

Unfortunately not all Team Briefing systems work well (or at all). Most failures happen because of one of the following two reasons.

1. Lack of perceived relevance. The Briefer may appreciate the relevance of a certain point but fail to make it clear to the team. People lose interest if the briefing has no obvious effect on them.

2. Lack of action following feedback. The most common form of feedback is questions. Sometimes Briefers don't know all the answers and have to make a promise to 'get back later' about something. Failure to keep these promises causes less and less feedback from the team. Once briefing becomes a monologue its potential to create understanding reduces considerably.

UNDER PERFORMANCE

While some of these problems may be caused by an overlong or irrelevant core brief, they can also be caused by poor performance on the part of the Briefer. It should be recognised that not all the nation's Team Briefers are well trained, enlightened leaders.

To some people, briefing is just another tedious task. They see it as a distraction from what they may regard as their real work.

MIXED MESSAGES

If Briefers perceive that their boss's priority is to maximise production, reduce costs or whatever, and that things like employee involvement are secondary considerations, they will naturally follow this example. It is not good enough for bosses to say they believe the right things, they must also demonstrate what they are committed to. It is not good enough for managers to make a passionate, rousing speech once in a while and then to revert back to standard behaviours. People react to and copy what they see to be the underlying management or cultural style.

If the senior management team don't actually believe that through effective communication employee involvement is cost effective, they should not try to run a Team Briefing process. It will not be durable in the long term.

PRACTICAL ACTIONS

Listed next are some tried and tested actions to demonstrate commitment and maintain the briefing process in good condition.

CHECK LOCAL BRIEFS

All Briefers should make notes through the month of points to brief. It is worth checking, halfway through the briefing cycle, what preparation has been done. This should be a supportive and not punitive activity. It should be done over and over again until the procedure is established and reliable. Briefers' managers should be looking for evidence of quality preparation and should not accept any excuses. They should not accept statements such as 'It's all in my head', unless that person is known to possess the gift of total recall.

WALK THE JOB

Senior managers should be visible and approachable. They should actually plan and diarise time to visit people at their workplace. This is very different from saying 'my door is always open' (which mainly causes draughts and interruptions).

It is often very difficult for a senior person to start a conversation with a junior person whom they hardly know. Like everything else it becomes easier with practice, but here are a few good 'icebreakers':

> 'How is it going here?'
> 'What's new around here?'
> 'What do you think of . . . .?'
> 'What projects are you working on?'
> 'When you were last briefed, what did you think regarding . . . .?'

This sort of approach never wears out, does not undermine anyone and tests people's understanding of what's going on. Well briefed people should be quite able to answer these kinds of questions.

A word of warning. If they have been briefed along the lines . . . . 'activity is up 17.96% on budget and 21.62% on this time last year', then a good response should be something like 'we're doing really well.'

If two or more people from a particular briefing team give unsatisfactory answers, it is worth asking the same questions of their Briefer. This will soon pinpoint the deficiency.

Briefers should be able to demonstrate their knowledge of the briefing system and how it is working in their area. They should be able, for instance, to state examples of what kind of things the team react best/worse to and the issues which create the most discussion etc.

SITTING IN

A natural extension of this theme is for senior Briefers is to sit in on briefings at the front end. An intention to do this must be well known in advance so that it does not come as a shock when it happens. There is no need to give the team concerned much notice. Whilst sitting in, the senior person should respect 'the chair' at all times. Some people initially find it unnerving to have a senior person present in a Team Briefing. However, most people find it works well and soon come to appreciate it, provided everyone feels able to act correctly and normally.

UNION REPRESENTATIVES/OTHER CONSULTATIVE BODIES

Representative bodies should provide feedback to senior management on the employees' perception of the Brief. Managers should seek this if it is not offered.

EMPLOYEE SURVEYS

More and more organisations are conducting Communication or Attitude Surveys on a regular basis. This not only shows the present state of affairs, but whether things are perceived to be getting better or worse.

THE CO-ORDINATOR/FEEDBACK FORMS

This one is last but not least. It is last because the Co-ordinator can only observe and advise. Accountability for good briefing goes with the management line. It cannot be driven by, for example, the Human Resources department.

It is not least because a good Co-ordinator can monitor Feedback Forms and flag up problems early on. They can often steer senior managers to give support where it is most needed.

SUMMARY

A former director of The Industrial Society once summarised management monitoring perfectly. He said that there were three kinds of jobs most likely to be done well at work.

They were:

1. Things people enjoy doing.

2. Things people are good at.

3. Things the boss checks up on.

This speaks volumes in connection with monitoring Team Briefing. Within organisations a great deal of time and energy is expended on checking and policing systems, performance, procedures and processes. We monitor output and progress as a matter of fundamental routine and when things are found to be working below par, or not at all, then corrections are made. TEAM BRIEFING SHOULD BE NO DIFFERENT.

The system itself needs to be examined at every level. Team Briefing needs to be the subject of routine discussion in management. Those who have other Briefers reporting to them should check the performance of their line Briefers. They should also 'leap-frog' and check further down the teams as part of regular routine walkabouts.

Team Briefing should be on the agenda at meetings of the Directorate – perhaps quarterly. Each director should be in a position to provide a two or three minute summary of how the process is working within his/her division or wing of the organisation. Establishing this as a standard routine will also ensure that checking and monitoring in each division becomes standard practice. Managers have to be accountable for Team Briefing.

There is also a case for including on job descriptions the requirement to undertake briefings. If this is done then Briefers will recognise the importance the organisation attaches to Team Briefing.

If there is also an Appraisal System in place which is intended to evaluate people's performance regarding their written accountabilities, then it follows that once Team Briefing *as an accountability* is on the job description, evaluation of performance in connection with it will occur naturally. No one can ever successfully evaluate someone's performance without regular checking and monitoring.

Essentially, Team Briefing monitoring should check:

- the relevance of what is being disseminated

- the speed and throughput of the process

- the management of the feedback process

- the performance of briefers

- people's levels of understanding

- for any misrepresentation of information

- that everyone is being briefed

- that briefings are not being deferred

- for adherence to standards

- that people who missed briefings through absence are subsequently briefed

Monitoring is a control mechanism. It is an ongoing month by month requirement. Additionally perhaps once or twice a year, Team Briefing should undergo the equivalent of a major 24,000 mile car service. Things should be put under the microscope and scrutinised.

The Industrial Society and some external consultancies will undertake such an audit on behalf of an organisation in an objective and unbiased way. This also adds the advantage that shortcomings can be reported without fear or favour, and without regard for any internal politics.

THE CO-ORDINATOR

It is extremely unlikely that an organisation should need to recruit externally an individual specially to become the Co-ordinator for Team Briefing. It is not a full-time job.

Increasingly, as organisations appoint employee communications professionals, based either in HR or corporate communications, these people are taking responsibility for team briefing co-ordination.

If there is no employee communications manager, someone should be selected who is already a high profile person and who understands not only what the organisation does, but, more importantly, the way it operates. It is usually someone who is highly regarded by people at all levels and who knows how to get things done.

ACCOUNTABILITIES

Some of the accountabilities of the Co-ordinator have already been mentioned. In summary they are:

- planning and structuring
- designing paperwork/briefers manuals
- training
- feedback
- publicity
- monitoring
- help/advisory

Much of the work of the Co-ordinator will be undertaken before Team Briefing actually goes live within the organisation. Thereafter, it becomes a question of maintenance, monitoring and dealing with anything which might go awry with the process and cause it to go off the rails.

STRUCTURE CHART

The Co-ordinator should draw up the Team Briefing structure chart for the organisation. *Everyone* must be briefed. We must look out for those who perhaps do not fit in to a natural affinity team and account for them as briefees.

Those who work in matrices and anyone who does not fit in the natural order of things have to be identified and their Briefer designated.

In cases where there are, for example, many management layers, it may be both possible and sensible to structure Team Briefing so that the briefing (cycle) can be speeded up. Groups of people can be combined for briefing purposes but only if they have work affinity and they can relate directly to the Briefer.

This may bring about cases where one Briefer briefs three or four very small teams, only one of which reports directly in to him or her. If so, the peer leaders of the other teams could conduct briefing for the combined teams in rotation, say one month on and two off. A little imagination and flexibility may be needed.

DESIGNING PAPERWORK

This is a relatively straightforward matter. The three example forms shown as appendices 1, 2 and 3 (Barclays Financial Services), are typical of those in use in many organisations. They are highly practical, thoughtfully customised and are used in the interests of keeping everything tidy. Additionally, the Feedback Form could be produced in self-carbonising sets of three. This can save both time and money on photocopying for distribution which would otherwise be necessary.

Providing each Briefer with a customised A4 ring binder to act as a training aide memoire and also as a storage file is well worth considering. These may contain advice regarding the structures, briefing instructions and permanent reminders (training handouts) about Team Briefing and how the process should work.

Briefers may also use it to store past copies of the briefing forms, perhaps for six months or so. This is practical and helpful because both Briefers and their briefees will sometimes want to check back on past briefing subjects. To have everything in one file seems sensible.

TRAINING FOR TEAM BRIEFING

The Co-ordinator may work in conjunction with those in Training Department and Human Resources to identify all who will need training for team briefing.

He or she may also input directly at training courses, whether conducted by external professionals or purely by internal trainers. In either case, the training should ideally be conducted in-house, something which the Co-ordinator could organise. Any direct input might include a module outlining the role of the Co-ordinator and generally support the key training initiative.

Induction Training is yet another consideration. Newly appointed staff should be informed about Team Briefing and its purposes. The Co-ordinator is the ideal person to undertake a session at Induction Courses.

OTHER ACCOUNTABILITIES

To sit-in on a sample of briefings to check on visual aids, timing, relevance, feedback and correct representation of the briefing topics.

Check the content of the Core Management Brief. It is important that it is always topical, not jargonised or unduly lengthy. (The 30/70 principle)

To check if line managers are sitting in. Perhaps this needs to be diarised.

Encouraging senior managers to walk-the-job, primarily to check that briefing is working according to plan. This too could be diarised.

To publicise Team Briefing. This may include any advance publicity but also regular updates in any in-house magazines or newspapers. Providing Team Briefing feedback publicity is also worth considering. A matter which may crop up in isolation in one individual team may be found to have significance for the entire workforce. Where a co-ordinator has a wider responsibility for employee communication, he/she can use newsletters, notices EMail or the house journal to publicize the question and answer.

To encourage the most senior management team to discuss Team Briefing – perhaps quarterly at the regular meetings of the Directorate.

To set up regular reviews of Team Briefing, by holding a meeting with a few managers, perhaps also quarterly.

The Co-ordinator must **have direct access to the Chief Executive**. This will facilitate any remedial action which may be needed from time to time. It will also enable the Co-ordinator to provide the CE with a summary of the feedback emanating from each briefing cycle. This is a very important part of the Team Briefing process.

From time to time they may need to make suggestions to the Chief Executive, for example over rumours circulating to which a response should be made, or persuading the CE to be more open about future plans.

SUMMARY

The Co-ordinator should **be the conscience of the process of Team Briefing**. He or she should become regarded as the focal reference point for any matter connected with Team Briefing.

Good Co-ordinators routinely provide advice and guidance to those who need it. Some even assist in the ongoing coaching of Briefers They give initial life to the process of Team Briefing and do everything possible to maintain it.

In large organisations, it may be necessary to 'appoint' more than one Co-ordinator – perhaps one for each division, or each major part of a company.

If so, then the Co-ordinating team will need to get together for a scheduled monthly meeting following each briefing cycle. They will need to establish a means of jointly co-ordinating the feedback and it may then be wise to determine whether or not there is also a need to appoint a Lead Co-ordinator from their number.

If divisional Co-ordinators are necessary in order to share the workload, then direct access to the divisional directors also becomes an important consideration.

The initial planning stages of Team Briefing will involve a great deal of time. It may be that the Co-ordinator(s) need to spend up to 20 hours a week solely dedicated to the design stages. Subsequently, once the process is up and running and it has been effectively monitored during its infancy, it is more likely that between 5 and 10 hours each week becomes the norm. Obviously, much will depend upon the number of teams and the scale of Team Briefing. This will vary from company to company.

APPENDICES

117

APPENDIX 1 SURVEY AND STATISTICAL ANALYSES

During 1994, The Industrial Society undertook a major survey of 915 organisations in the British Isles in connection with Employee Communications.

Amongst some of the very revealing findings were that:

- Nearly 75% of employers had no written policy on internal communications.

- Approximately only one third of organisations linked employee communications policy to the strategic business plan.

- Almost three quarters of organisations had no specific budget for employee communications.

- Notice boards, Team Briefing and Newsletters were the most commonly used downward communication channels.

- Team Briefing was seen as easily the most EFFECTIVE channel for communicating with employees.

- 'Walking-the-job' and Team Briefing feedback were the most widely used 'upward' communication channels.

- Judged on effectiveness, Team Briefing feedback was the highest rated 'upward' communication channel.

- One in four organisations made no attempt to measure the effectiveness of their employee communication activity.

The following two analyses summarise findings regarding both downward and upward employee communications.

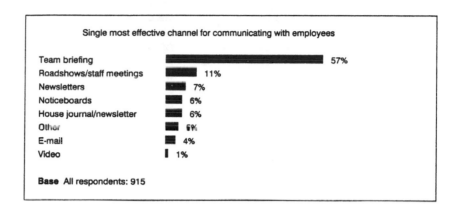

The following chart summarises the perceived effectiveness from the means of listening to employees.

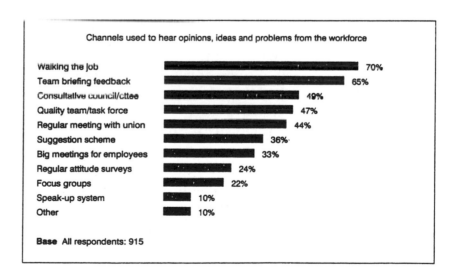

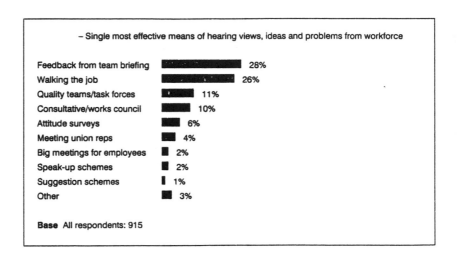

– Single most effective means of hearing views, ideas and problems from workforce

Feedback from team briefing	28%
Walking the job	26%
Quality teams/task forces	11%
Consultative/works council	10%
Attitude surveys	6%
Meeting union reps	4%
Big meetings for employees	2%
Speak-up schemes	2%
Suggestion schemes	1%
Other	3%

Base All respondents: 915

These findings place a great deal of emphasis upon Team Briefing, both from the point of view of downward and upward communication. In 82% of the organisations there exists a process of Team Briefing.

We also know that the medium of Team Briefing is used in some organisations in other countries. Companies in the USA, Africa, Australia, Holland, Germany and France have asked The Industrial Society for help in establishing Team Briefing in recent times. Some organisations in the U.K. which are owned by Japanese conglomerates also use Team Briefing.

In the Republic of Ireland, an organisation which uses Team Briefing as part of an overall company wide communications strategy has achieved remarkable success directly through the process.

APPENDIX II THE IRISH PERMANENT BUILDING SOCIETY

With its head offices in Dublin, has 100 branches throughout the British Isles. It is a major Financial Services organisation with a turnover of £82 (I.R.) millions annually. Some 12 000 people are employed in locations throughout the British Isles.

The company employs a small team of people dedicated to internal communications headed by an Internal Communications Manager.

The following is an account of what the organisation, with a diverse and widely scattered workforce, has done to address communications:

STRATEGY

Irish Permanent's current internal communications' set-up dates from an initiative in 1991. At the first ever general meeting for all employees, new Chief Executive Roy Douglas announced that a new internal communications policy statement would be circulated to staff. Prior to that, all managers had taken part in an eight-week Team Briefing programme.

Before this, employee communications were patchy and lacked co-ordination. Staff were frequently in the dark about what was going on in the Society and were without information they needed to do their jobs effectively.

The Society makes a definite, explicit link between corporate business strategy and its communications with staff – recognising the contribution that a well-informed and motivated staff can make to the overall success of the business. The topic is regularly on Board agendas, while major individual initiatives such as the staff survey (see below) receive full Board presentations.

The commitment to internal communications has delivered business benefits through a well–informed staff, the Society believes. Staff in Irish Permanent now expect to be kept informed of all developments and this has created a momentum that would be difficult, and undesirable, to stop.

TEAM BRIEFING

Irish Permanent made downward communication the top initial priority – with a new Team Briefing system as the hub of its initiative.

From the start of the communications drive in 1991 the Society closed all branches for half an hour once a month, at the start of the day, for Team Briefing.

With the success of the initiative, managers now often allow longer for the briefing process. The system is a relatively formal and regulated one. The internal communications manager works directly with the Chief Executive and the senior management team to develop the monthly Core Brief.

Fears that closing branches during work hours for Team Briefing would damage business have proved unfounded. The actual impact, which the Society has researched, has been 'minimal, minuscule' from the point of view of customer satisfaction.

Irish Permanent has recently carried out an evaluation, with staff, regarding the effectiveness of its Team Briefing. It became apparent from this that employees were coming to work early on Team Briefing days in order to allow more time for discussion. The Society is now experimenting with an extra closure time for staff meetings.

CONSULTATION

Drawing on the success of the Team Briefing system, Irish Permanent is now planning to close branches for another part-morning in the month in order to launch a pre-decision consultation system with staff.

The Society consults unions (MSF and a management association) on routine issues.

CORPORATE VALUES WORKSHOPS

Since the end of 1992, groups of employees have participated in regular three-day workshops, at a single location, focusing on 'core values' identified in a staff consultative exercise: customer service, professionalism, profitability and teamwork. The results were brought together in booklet form and made available to all employees.

Developed by Irish Permanent's 'values teams' and facilitated by a training consultant, each workshop involves a 'diagonal' section of the workforce – i.e. from different levels and locations in the company – and over 18 months will cover all employees.

DOCUMENTS

A range of regular and ad hoc documents underpin Irish Permanent's employee communications. The documents have a co-ordinated, corporate look – a product of a deliberate decision to go for high quality communications materials, now produced on relatively low cost in-house DTP facilities. All design of materials was done in-house.

IRISH PERMANENT NEWS

A regular 12–page colour tabloid newspaper, distributed to all employees, reporting business, general and social news.

THE IP BULLETIN

Produced by the internal communications team, this bulletin is delivered to each Irish Permanent office every Thursday morning. The bulletin resembles a newspaper, is inviting to read and covers stories of interest and importance to all parts of Irish Permanent. As a result, it is widely accepted and read throughout the Society.

The 2–4 page A4 bulletin, which carries staff notices and 'social' information, has streamlined the communications process by reducing the number of internal communications documents.

PRIORITY BRIEF

Produced when needed, this Brief updates staff, via managers, on important developments in the business before, or no later than, the media and major clients and customers. The Society rates the effectiveness of this Brief very highly, and it is continually under review.

INTERNAL COMMUNICATIONS DOCUMENTS

Referenced and numbered, this regular series of documents – usually covering one or two topics only – collates product, operational and marketing information being produced by different departments to ensure maximum lateral awareness of what is going on in the business.

The initiative cut by some 60% the amount of paper circulating round the organisation, as well as increasing staff confidence in the information they receive.

SATELLITE NETWORK

The Society has just installed a satellite network capable of broadcasting to all offices simultaneously. After booking a time slot on the satellite, from fifteen minutes upwards, the Society transmits from a Dublin studio across a network protected from unauthorised access by a security system. Amongst other things, the Society expects to use the network to complement the Team Briefing system

STAFF SURVEY

Irish Permanent sees its regular staff survey as a critical part of the communications flow, helping to clarify staff views on specifics and so strengthening the decision making process. At the last survey in February 1993 the response rate was 87%.

In order to communicate the results of the survey:

- **all staff received a summary of the results;**

- **all department heads got the full report, which was available on request to employees;**

- **the Chief Executive and a director led staff 'roadshows' at the company's seven main**

locations to present and discuss the survey results;

- **verbatim comments made in the survey were made available to the management team, but not to all employees.**

One direct outcome of the staff attitude survey has been a 'customer service improvement study' – a project that brings in staff from all levels to look at suggestions for enhancing service to the Society's customers.

The project allows any employee to feed suggestions via a telephone 'helpdesk' to a central project team meeting once a month.

Apart from the staff attitude survey, the internal communications team have done mini-surveys such as Team Briefing evaluation, and a survey of staff queries about Irish Permanent's conversion to plc status. Results were used to develop 'roadshow' presentations throughout the Society by senior executives.

COMMUNICATIONS TRAINING

All Irish Permanent's managers – including the Chief Executive – receive training, via the Training and Development department, in briefing skills. The company is now planning to establish a rolling programme to regularise the process.

COMMUNICATIONS FUNCTION

Irish Permanent has a single Internal Communications Manager, reporting to the General Manager for management services. The very small internal communications team is supplemented by a growing number of information providers across the Irish Permanent network, as 'ownership' of the communications process spreads.

BEST PRACTICE

The three most important ingredients of the Societys communications policy are:

1. (To quote the Societys own internal communications policy): 'Responsibility for internal communications lies with each and every individual and not with any specific department or particular individual.'

2. Top management commitment to good communications.

3. A firm, formal Team Briefing system.

SUMMARY

Irish Permanent's efforts to successfully manage internal communications are impressive. The performance of the organisation and employee involvement are seen to be directly linked, evidencing the belief that a well informed workforce is a better workforce. Things are never perfect of course, and their constant examination and re-examination of communications aimed at continuous improvement is an excellent example of good management practice.

●I gratefully acknowledge the permission granted to me by The Irish Permanent Building Society, to produce this Case Study.

APPENDIX III BARCLAYS FINANCIAL SERVICES LIMITED

APPENDIX 1
BARCLAYS FINANCIAL SERVICES LIMITED

FEEDBACK FORM

Briefing Team _____ *Team Briefer* _____

Date of Briefing _____ *Time* _____

List of questions outstanding from last month

List of unanswered questions

REMEMBER IT IS YOUR RESPONSIBILITY TO FIND OUT AND REPORT BACK ANSWERS TO THESE QUESTIONS

QUESTIONS SHOULD BE ANSWERED WITHIN 5 WORKING DAYS OF THE BRIEFING

Brief note on questions asked

What was of most interest to your team?

Positive suggestions made

Copies to be sent to i) Review Group Co-ordinator and ii) Immediate Manager.
Original copy to be retained by Team Briefer.

APPENDIX 2
BARCLAYS FINANCIAL SERVICES LIMITED

MANAGEMENT CORE BRIEF

Date brief prepared

Originator/s

Note to Team Briefer

1. *This brief provides the core message - add this information to your own briefing material.*

2. *Convey the meaning in your own words, which you know will be understood, and where possible illustrate with a practical example that is relevant to your team.*

3. *Words or phrases which need to convey a precise meaning will be underlined. These should not be changed in briefing.*

4. *Encourage questions. If you do not know the answer, say so, make a note, get the answer and give it to the questioner at the earliest possible time.*

5. *Ensure that you have prepared your own local brief, and have it checked by your manager, before he/she briefs you.*

Subjects and key points

Additional information/notes

APPENDIX 3
BARCLAYS FINANCIAL SERVICES LIMITED

LOCAL BRIEF

Team Briefer	*Names of those absent*
Department/Section	
Date & Time of Briefing	
Brief originated by	

Subjects and key points	*Notes, giving examples and answers to possible questions*